icebreaker

sixth edition

icebreaker

a manual for public speaking

sixth edition

Tracey L. Smith
Lewis and Clark Community College

Mary Tague-Busler
Lewis and Clark Community College

WAVELAND
PRESS, INC.
Long Grove, Illinois

For information about this book, contact:
Waveland Press, Inc.
4180 IL Route 83, Suite 101
Long Grove, IL 60047-9580
(847) 634-0081
info@waveland.com
www.waveland.com

Cover graphic: © IMAGEZOO/SuperStock

10-digit ISBN 1-57766-615-1
13-digit ISBN 978-1-57766-615-8

Printed in the United States of America

7   6   5   4

To our daughters,
Ashley and Jessica Smith, and
Nicole and Kelsey Busler.
You are our inspiration.
We know you have had to live and breathe communication
your whole lives, but we think it was well worth it.
You are successful students, mothers, workers, women, and people.
We are so proud of all of you!

Contents

Preface

This edition of *Icebreaker* has some distinctive changes from previous editions. The entire chapter format has changed. The text is now organized into twelve chapters. Each chapter begins with chapter highlights aimed at giving readers a comprehensive overview of what they will learn. We introduce each chapter with the story of John and Pam, two ordinary working adults. Through their experiences, readers gain insight into how the information presented in each chapter relates to a real-life situation. We have retained the "Application to Everyday Life" examples because they provide the opportunity to use the concepts discussed in each chapter. We also include "Strengthen Your Skills" exercises within each chapter so that readers can practice essential elements of public speaking. Changes incorporated in the sixth edition have evolved from our own experience in using the text in both higher education classes and business training sessions. We have also included information based on comments and suggestions offered by our colleagues and users of the previous edition. We are very excited about the final product!

Textbook revisions are a difficult and time-consuming process. We would like to thank our families, friends, and colleagues for their patience and understanding during the revision of this textbook. We would also like to thank our students for their continued support and suggestions. Finally, to you our readers, we thank you for taking the time to improve your public speaking skills through the use of this text. It is you whom we envisioned as we worked to create a clear and comprehensive overview of the speech process. We hope this sixth edition of *Icebreaker: A Manual for Public Speaking* continues to provide you with clear instruction on how to prepare and deliver speeches, and help students understand the importance of public speaking and feel comfortable in becoming proficient at it.

1

Is It Really Worth It?

An Introduction to Speaking

- Communicating requires the ability to exchange our thoughts, feelings, and ideas.
- Communication requires us to share information through speech.
- Oral communication has been used in many cultures throughout history.
- In a democratic society we can freely communicate our ideas to one another.
- Everyday conversations are much like formal public speaking.
- Daily communication requires the effective exchange of ideas and feelings.
- The communication process is best understood by using a simple model.
- Many times the message sent is not the message received.
- There are three general reasons why this may occur.
- Being aware of how communication occurs will help you be an effective speaker.

John is nervous. He is waiting patiently in the lobby area of the vice president's office. He has been called to the office for a special meeting by the VP himself. John is not sure what to expect. The company has many vice presidents both male and female. This particular man is in charge of employee benefits and relations. John is not really sure what that means or how it relates to his job in sales. He is getting more nervous by the minute.

Pam is also nervous. She, too, is waiting in the lobby for the same meeting. She has never met the Vice President of Employee Relations. She is excited and apprehensive. She was asked to come to a special meeting today. She has no idea what the meeting is about. She wonders if it has anything to do with her new position in the Marketing and Advertising Department.

Vice President Al Jones is in his office finishing up a conference call with all the VPs from other company offices nationwide. He is pleased with the outcome and the decision they have made together. He presses the intercom button on his desk and asks his assistant to send in John and Pam. It's time to get the ball rolling.

Pam and John are asked by the assistant to enter the office together. They both think this is interesting and unusual. They have never met one another, and the fact that they are entering the meeting together causes some alarm. They enter, are greeted by Al, and the meeting begins. One hour later, John and Pam leave Al's office with a new assignment. They are to jointly plan a large conference. This is the first time that two executives, let alone a male and female, have been placed in charge of the annual corporate meeting. This meeting brings together employees from all geographic locations and covers many areas nationwide. The annual meeting takes place in an entire weekend and all departments are highlighted. The meeting involves business, recreation, and networking. This is the singular most important event the company hosts each year. John and Pam are excited and honored that they have been chosen to plan such an important event. They make plans to meet over lunch the next day to start discussing ideas for the event.

John walks away thinking that this is the best assignment he has ever been given. Not only will he get a break from sales and traveling for awhile, the assignment will be a breeze. He has planned numerous sales events in the past and even plans his annual family reunion. This should be no problem. After all, aren't all get-togethers basically the same?

Pam returns to her office lost in thought. What a huge task she has just been given! Not only must information be prepared for all the employees of the company, but she and John must address recreational activities, food, and lodging as well. The planning alone will be tremendous, not to mention the event itself. She is glad she and John are meeting for lunch tomorrow so that they can talk about their ideas early. The last time she helped plan an event it was a disaster. This could be a communication nightmare!

We know the course will be easier for you if you can find relevant use for the course content. Therefore, throughout the text you will find the story of John and Pam. We will follow these two executives as they plan their company's annual conference. This, in addition to the "Strengthen Your Skills" and "Application to Everyday Life" boxes, will help you examine how the principles, concepts, and skills being discussed in the text can be applied to your own lives.

We often do not realize how important communication is in our daily lives. Communicating with others on a daily basis requires the ability to exchange our thoughts, feelings, and ideas. To function in society, you must be able to get your messages across to all kinds of people in many different types of situations. How do you explain your project to your boss at work? How can you get the mechanic to understand what that funny noise is in your car? How do you get your kids to clean their rooms? How do you ask for the help you need from a friend? These are only a few instances where good communication skills are essential.

The Importance of Communication

Some of the skills you have used in these everyday conversations are similar to those that you will learn for public speaking. The skills you learn in this class will help you in your personal, professional, and civic life. Although you may not think you will ever give a speech in "real life," you will be involved in many situations every day that require you to share information orally with others through speech.

Oral communication has been used throughout history in many cultures. These societies believed that the ability to speak effectively in public was critical to the success of their respective way of life. The ancient Greeks and Romans believed that effective oration, the ability to speak well in public, was crucial to their political and educational framework. Over the centuries there have been many men and women who have shared their visions with the world from the podium. Some of these notable speakers are Abraham Lincoln, Dale Carnegie, Martin Luther King Jr., Billy Graham, Margaret Thatcher, and Princess Diana. Public speaking is an important means for sharing information. It can help people increase their feelings of individual self-worth, enhance their professional life, and even help them participate in government.

In the United States, we live in a democratic society that allows freedom of speech. Therefore, we have a collective responsibility as members of this type of society to participate in our democratic government. As individuals of a democracy, we can freely communicate our ideas to one another. This can

Abraham Lincoln successfully rallied support through his public speeches.

be accomplished through the skill of public speaking. In public speaking, you can share your ideas and opinions and can learn to be a critical thinker and listener. This skill can help you to make informed decisions about our government. The authors of the Constitution knew the importance of citizen participation and educated decision making. They provided a framework for a democracy unlike any other in the world. It is our responsibility to continue to make it work. What you learn from a course in public speaking can make you a better citizen and a skilled, functioning member of our society. Hence, the goal of a public speaking course is to provide you with the skills necessary to achieve success in all aspects of your life, including your civic responsibilities. Imagine the feeling of accomplishment you will have as you realize that you can effectively express your beliefs in a discussion of public issues.

Public speaking requires you to be able to share your feelings or opinions with others. Sometimes you have to share information, facts, or figures, and other times you may have to persuade another person to accept your viewpoint. Communication in this form is not manipulation of others; you are merely explaining your point of view with enough support to allow another person to see things your way. As you gain support for your way of thinking, your confidence will grow and your ability to explain yourself will improve.

There are many situations that occur on a daily basis that require you to provide information or be persuasive. Let's say you are seated in a meeting of your Parent–Teacher Organization when someone suggests that the group spend $10,000 to build a new playground. You believe that the money could be better spent acquiring more computers for classrooms. You could sit in that meeting muttering under your breath to your neighbor in the next seat, or you could seek recognition from the chairperson and explain your objections to the whole assembled group. Chances are that there will be others in the assembly who feel as you do but lack the courage to stand and provide information about the new computers or to persuade the group that spending the money on a playground is unwise.

Even if you are not a member of a Parent–Teacher Organization, you converse with others every day. Everyday conversations are much like formal public speaking. As a human being, you experience a whole range of feelings. You possess the intelligence and ability to share these feelings with others through the use of language. Daily conversations about meals, chores, and errands require you to interact with others through the power of speech. We accomplish this by organizing our thoughts into coherent messages that we transmit to other individuals. We often do this vocally and then wait for a response. We communicate in this fashion with our families and friends. Not only does your daily life rely on speech, but your outside interests and profession will demand that you be able to communicate daily in various situations.

Daily communication requires the efficient and effective exchange of ideas and feelings between and among people. Public speaking is based on the same principles. It doesn't matter whether you are deciding what activity

Our daily conversations with others involve many of the same elements used in public speaking.

to do this weekend or you are in a board meeting presenting an explanation of an audit report; getting your ideas and viewpoints across to another person or persons requires the same skills for both situations.

Perhaps an analogy will help clarify this message. Speaking to a group of friends versus speaking to an assembled work group is analogous to the similarities and differences between writing a personal letter and writing a business letter. For both types of letters, your goal is to share information. The differences occur only in the specific form that the letter takes. In an informal letter to a friend you might not be concerned with sentence structure, spelling, or punctuation. You might refer to examples without explaining them, or use slang terms that you and your friend share. In a business letter you would be very concerned with the grammar, spelling, and punctuation. You would also be sure to use words properly and in their correct form and structure. An informal discussion with friends versus a formal speech or discussion is very similar to this letter-writing example. Essentially the difference is one of form, not purpose. Consequently, the skills you learn in a public speaking class can easily be transferred to your general interpersonal communication, resulting in fewer misunderstandings and clearer messages being delivered.

The Process of Communication

Before you can learn to speak more effectively in any communication situation, understanding the elements of communication is necessary. *Communication* is the process of thinking and feeling, receiving and conveying messages to ourselves and others in a manner that brings ideas and people together. The communication process is best understood by using a simple model. A *model* is a simplified representation that is used to understand a more complex device, process, or concept. The diagram on the following page illustrates the communication process and shows areas where it can become confusing or less effective. Being aware of these areas will help you, as a *communicator,* deliver and receive messages more effectively. To illustrate this process, we will use a simple communication model. This model attempts to freeze a split second in the communication process so that we can see what is happening.

Experiences have happened to us from the day we were born. These experiences are stored in our brain and play a role in shaping how we think and feel. These experiences create who we are and how we view the world. In communication we call these collective experiences our *personal environment.* In order to communicate effectively with someone else, we must isolate those experiences that relate to what we want to convey to others. This is necessary to help us form a message that another person can understand.

The first step in sending a message actually occurs when a person (communicator 1) has an idea, opinion, or feeling and wants to let another person (communicator 2) know about it. When we experience a thought, we do not initially think about it in words, but experience it as a mental image or *symbol.* For example, let's say you want to ask someone to see a movie with you Friday night. The beginning of this idea occurs with your mind "seeing" you and your friend at the theater. The process of turning a mental image into a symbol is called *encoding.* Once you have completed this encoding process you have a message to send to another person. The *message* is the symbol or idea you want the other person to understand. Your encoded message must travel through some medium or *channel.* The channel may be used for *verbal elements,* which refer to spoken or written language, or *nonverbal elements,* such as posture, facial expressions, eye contact, or even the manner in which we say our words.

Once the encoded message travels through its channel, it arrives at its destination, communicator 2. This is the person whom you want to understand what you are attempting to communicate. Since communication consists of sending and receiving messages, listening is another essential component in the process. *Listening* is the psychological process of understanding the message after the physical process of *hearing* has occurred. Communicator 2 must listen to the message and make a conscious psychological effort to turn the message back into a mental image. The process of turning a

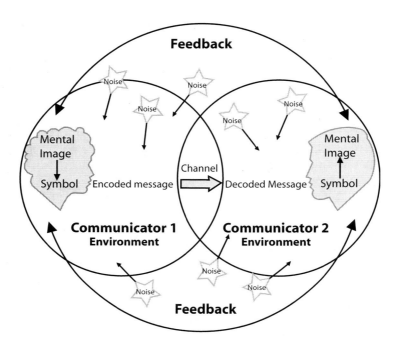

message that has been received back into a mental image, or symbol, is called *decoding.* This process is the same whether you are speaking to one or several people. Therefore, the model is representative of a conversation between two people or a speaker delivering a speech to an audience of fifty people. While this may appear to be a linear process (the message starting at point 1 and ending at point, 2), communication is really a simultaneous process. This is because both communicators are sending their messages back and forth to each other at the same time. In our example, John is probably watching communicator 1 while she is asking him to go to a movie. The fact that he is using eye contact, a form of nonverbal communication, while she is speaking makes his message occur simultaneously to hers. This constant exchange of messages results in what is called *feedback.* Feedback can be verbal or nonverbal and is what makes communication a two-way process.

Many times the message sent (encoded) is not the message received (decoded). For example, let's say you (communicator 1) want to describe a square to another person. You choose the words to send your message, but when communicator 2 decodes your message, his or her mental image is of a rectangle, not a square. Why did this happen? Obviously the message sent was not the message received. By looking at what actually causes ineffective communication, we can lessen the likelihood of the message being misunderstood.

    1. The encoded message was unclear. The first reason that a message is misunderstood is because the encoded message was unclear. When you do not clearly encode your message, the other person cannot understand what you mean. There are many reasons why a message may not be clearly encoded. We might leave out important information in our verbal communication. This means that the words chosen to represent our mental images were not detailed enough to be understood by the receiver of the message. Maybe I ask you to take the trash out today. When I come home the trash is still in the house. I am angry because you did not do as I asked. You don't understand. It is only 2:00 PM and there is still a lot of time "today" to take out the trash. My omission of a specific time "today" to take out the trash in an encoded message caused you to misunderstand the message. Another reason a message might be unclear is if the receiver misinterpreted the nonverbal communication in my encoded message. For example, I might choose to use a gesture to communicate. I raise one finger causing you to think I want one piece of bread, but I am really gesturing for you to wait a moment while I decide. Effective communication requires a complete and clear message to be developed in the encoding process before it is sent, verbally or nonverbally. Otherwise, it is likely that miscommunication may occur.

2. **The sender and receiver do not share the same personal environment.** The second cause of messages going astray is that the communicators may not share the same personal environments. Personal environments include everything that has been experienced by a person: education, religion, home atmosphere, historical background, moods, and so on (represented in the diagram as circles around the communicators). No two people share exactly the same personal environment. We are all individuals who are unique in many ways, although our environments can overlap in certain common areas. The shared parts of our environments can help us understand each other better. When our environments differ in an area we are trying to communicate about, very often communication becomes ineffective. An example of differing environments and the misunderstandings that occur might be as follows: The sender is awake and happy, while the receiver is tired and grouchy. The sender says, "Gee, you look attractive today," meaning it as a genuine compliment. The receiver, because of his or her different mood (environment), interprets this message as an insult and replies, "I suppose you mean I don't look good any other day!" The message sent obviously wasn't the message received, and miscommunication has occurred due to the different experience, or personal environments, of the two communicators.

3. **The receiver was distracted by noise.** The final cause of miscommunication is noise interfering with a person receiving a message. *Noise* is any distraction that hinders communication. Arrows on the model

represent the interference of noise. There are two general types of noise: external noise and internal noise. *External noise* can be audible sounds produced outside your ears—factory machinery in operation, telephones ringing, children arguing, televisions blaring, or other people talking—that make it difficult to concentrate. External noise can also include nonaudible interferences such as a hot room, an unpleasant odor, or an uncomfortable chair. External noise hinders our ability to hear or listen to what is being said. This may cause us to misinterpret all or part of the message being sent.

Internal noise is caused by the thoughts and feelings we are experiencing inside our minds or bodies. When your mind is preoccupied, such as with daydreaming or worrying about an exam, you are experiencing internal noise. Internal noise can also be caused by actual hearing problems or defects. A person who is hearing impaired—either permanently or temporarily, as from a bad cold—may find it difficult to understand a verbal message.

Any, all, or a combination of what causes ineffective communication may result in the message sent not being the message received. Being aware of how communication occurs and knowing where possible problems might arise will help you be a more effective speaker. This is true whether you are speaking to a friend, your family, your coworkers, or your public speaking class.

Strengthen Your Skills

Make Your Own Model

Purpose: The purpose of this exercise is to help you identify those areas where the message sent may go astray.

Procedure:

1. Collect magazines, scissors, paste, and markers.
2. Using your assembled materials, create your own communication model.
3. Clearly label those areas that we identified as areas where communication goes astray.
4. Practice giving a speech by explaining your model to your classmates.

Conclusion

We often take our communication for granted. Considering how important it is in our lives, this can be a problem. We've all experienced situations when we were misunderstood, the message we thought we sent was not interpreted in the manner we intended. Investing time and energy to learn how to be effective communicators will provide big payoffs in our lives.

Application to Everyday Life

Consider for a moment what our society would be like without effective communication. How would we exist? How would we connect with others? How would we have our needs met? What if we couldn't express our ideas, convictions, and hopes? Of course we do have the ability to communicate both verbally and nonverbally, yet our messages often go astray. Considering the importance that communication plays in our lives, don't you agree that it is worth the time and effort to become an effective speaker?

DISCUSSION QUESTIONS

1. What historical evidence is there that speaking effectively is an important skill valued by all cultures?

2. In what ways are speaking to your family and speaking to a larger audience the same? In what ways are they different?

3. What causes messages to go astray? Give an example from your own life that illustrates each and explain how they can be avoided in the future.

4. Explain the process of communication, giving illustrations or definitions for each step.

5. What do you think is your biggest problem when communicating with others? What are your strong points?

KEY WORDS

- channel
- communication
- communicator
- decoding
- encoding
- external noise
- feedback
- hearing
- internal noise
- listening
- message
- model
- noise
- nonverbal elements
- personal environment
- symbol
- verbal elements

2

Let's Talk!

Behind
the Podium

Chapter Highlights

- The goal of communication is to relay ideas in a way that is understandable to others.
- Effective speakers adapt their speaking skills to individual situations.
- In order to be an effective speaker, you need to create a working plan.
- A working plan will incorporate three elements: audience, occasion, and environment.
- Unexpected events can cause nervousness and speech anxiety.
- Understanding the reactions of your body when you are nervous or anxious can help you conquer speech anxiety.
- There are five tips that can help anxious speakers overcome speech anxiety.
- The CEM method is invaluable in helping beginning speakers overcome fear and build confidence.

Pam knows that when you are planning an event, either for business or pleasure, there's a period of time during which we anticipate everything that might happen or could go wrong. Will the event be successful? Will it satisfy everyone's needs (to relax or to secure a new client)? What decisions need to be made? What's essential to promote a sense of cohesion, and what should be done to prepare for her first meeting with John? Pam has decided that in order to prepare for this corporate event they will need a calendar so they can keep track of when significant details need to be completed. They must also work-in their day-to-day work schedule so that neither one of them gets behind in their regular duties. Pam is lost in thought, considering all the decisions that have to be made early in the planning process as to the types of materials that need to be presented at the conference and who would be best to deliver the various speeches.

Meanwhile, John is also lost in thought. He is making a list of the things that make get-togethers enjoyable. The family gatherings he has planned in the past have a little bit of everything. They are organized and designed so that everyone has something to do that appeals directly to their individual tastes and interests.

John makes sure there are activities, food, quiet time, and other special aspects so that the event can continue for a long time without anyone getting bored. He also recalls that there are many moments when someone in the family takes center stage to tell everyone gathered some amusing story or to relay some information about a relative who is sick or could not attend. They always have a planning session for next year's event. This is always challenging, as everyone has to be persuaded to keep the tradition alive and well. He begins to add these items to his growing list. He is thinking that, with a little bit of adaptation, these same elements can be addressed to make their conference successful and interesting to everyone in attendance. He is beginning to get excited with all of the possibilities. He wants to have his list completed in time to show to Pam at their meeting tomorrow. After all, if they have considered the audience, the reason for the meeting, and the physical location, planning the other elements should be easier.

We have already discussed the importance of communication in our lives. However, many of you may still not be convinced that the skills you learn in a public speaking class will ever be used again once you complete the course. In this chapter, we will discuss the importance of planning your speech, the presence of speech anxiety—and methods of dealing with it.

You Are a Speaker Every Day

The goal of communication is to relay your ideas in a way that is understandable to others. It doesn't matter if you are speaking to an audience of one or a thousand. When you attempt to communicate, you want the other person(s) to understand what you are saying. While there are some obvious differences between being the keynote speaker at a company's annual conference and talking to your five-year-old son, the general purpose is *exactly the same!* As the keynote speaker, your goal is for one-thousand audience members to comprehend your message. As a parent, your goal is for your son to understand your directions. The audiences and messages are different, but as the speaker, you apply the same concepts and skills to achieve understanding.

The skills necessary to deliver a speech can be used to tutor your child or help a sibling with her homework. They can make you a hero as you successfully talk a friend through a computer problem or provide instructions on home improvement. Now think about the persuasive skills you use in your everyday conversations. Wouldn't you like to be able to present your view in a such a way that others would consider them to be valuable? Need to convince your children that they should clean their rooms, or your parents to extend your curfew? The principles you will learn in this speaking course are exactly what you need to make these day-to-day communication situations successful. Hopefully you are beginning to see that being an effective speaker in any situation simply means adapting your speaking skills to individual situations. At the conclusion of this course, you should be a more effective speaker both publicly and privately.

Becoming an Effective Speaker Requires Planning

As we saw with the story of John and Pam at the beginning of the chapter, a successful event requires a lot of planning. Creating a speech for delivery to an audience is no different. In order to be an effective speaker, you need to create a plan. This **working plan** will define and incorporate three elements that will always be present during your speech: audience, occasion, and speaking environment. Careful study of and planning for all of these elements will make your job as speaker much easier. Let's examine each element more closely, beginning with the people in your audience. If you want to keep your audience members' attention while you are speaking, it is important to know as much information about them as possible.

Audience Members

You must first determine who the people are in your audience. What do they know? What do they believe? What are their personal characteristics, habits, or lifestyles? These questions can be answered by conducting a survey, called an **audience analysis** that contains questions that help you to learn more about your audience. These questions will help you to gather **demographic data**—measurable statistics such as age, gender, occupation, education, and income level—about your listeners as well as **psychological data**—measurable information about such characteristics as attitudes, morals, values, religious beliefs, and lifestyle. Gathering both types of information will help you to decide what to put in your speech that will be interesting to the people present. Audience analysis is a common method used throughout the retail goods industry to find out about consumer preferences. For example, have you ever gone to the mall and been asked to provide your zip code to the clerk at checkout as part of a survey being conducted by the store? Knowing their customers' zip codes is a way for that store to gather demographic information that can help determine the income levels and perhaps the lifestyles of the consumers who are shopping in their store. This information might help in product placement or in determining what products to carry, so that the store can cater to its customers. The audience analysis you complete for your speech is similar. You will ask your audience questions that will help you determine how to tailor your topic specifically to their needs and wants.

The information you gain in your audience analysis will help you understand your audience's desires so that you can speak directly to them. You will be gaining your listeners' interest by speaking about things that relate to their specific personal beliefs, experiences, knowledge, and lifestyle. For example, if you were giving a speech about saving money for retirement, the demographic and psychological data you would collect from a group of college students would be vastly different than that of a senior citizens' group! By asking questions of your audience you can determine if they are willing and motivated to listen to you. The answers or results you receive from your questions can be related specifically to your topic and used in your speech. This information will help you to eliminate or add information as you prepare your speech.

It is important to note that audiences can be both individual and collective. Often your group will respond as a whole (as when they are all college students). Sometimes they will respond as individuals (some are dental students, others history majors, etc.). This is often the case when psychological issues, such as morals and lifestyle, are surveyed. Here is an exercise to help you analyze your classroom audience.

Strengthen Your Skills

Audience Analysis

Purpose: To learn how to analyze your audience.

Procedure:

1. Your instructor will divide the class into groups of five to seven. Group members should discuss their individual demographic and psychological characteristics: age, income, religion, educational level, lifestyles, morals, etc.

2. The groups should have approximately twenty to thirty minutes for discussion.

3. After discussions, pool the information for the entire class and analyze the results.

4. The results should show the overall demographic and psychological characteristics of your class, therefore providing you with an "analysis" of your audience.

Now that you have done your first audience analysis of the members of your class, remember that you need to do this same process for any audience you may be asked to speak to, in or out of the classroom. By going through this process, you have prepared for the first element in the speaking process, *the audience.* Next, you must apply the information you have learned about your audience to the speaking occasion.

Occasion

The *occasion* for which you are speaking refers to the actual event requiring a speech. This event could be a company's annual conference, such as the one John and Pam are planning; a student senate meeting; a classroom presentation about a topic being studied by students; or a report to the budget-planning committee. Knowing why you and your audience are gathering will help you set the direction your speech should take and is the second element of your working plan. It is also important to know how much time has been allotted for your speech, and how much time is required for you to make all of your points. If you are asked to speak for ten minutes, your audience will expect you to speak that length of time, not less or more.

Time allotment may not seem like an important issue, but let's consider an example where proper planning for time may be the case. If you have been asked to speak for twenty minutes before dinner, you do not want to be speaking when the waiters appear with the first plates. Your speech should be concluded so that the audience may enjoy their meal. You do not want to ask the wait staff to hold the meal either, or the entire kitchen staff is inconvenienced. Think about meetings at work. Typically you will know how long to speak in such a situation from previous meetings. What happens if someone speaks longer? That's right, people tune out and start thinking about all the work they need to get back to or what they want for lunch. These are just two examples of why it is important to consider time in this step of your working plan. Time is often one of the most frustrating elements in your plan, because you must be organized enough to cover the material without exceeding the time allotted.

Once you have adequately determined why you are meeting and have planned for the length of your speech, you have completed the second element in your working plan. You are now ready to plan for the speaking environment.

Speaking Environment

The *speaking environment* is the third and final element of the working plan. The environment you will be speaking in consists of the facility and general area in which you will address your audience. Will you be speaking in a classroom, an intimate living room, at a conference table, or in a large auditorium? Will there be a podium, a microphone, a flip chart, or an overhead projector? What if you are demonstrating how to paint holiday ornaments? Are the necessary supplies, including water, accessible? Will the audience members be able to see you from their seats? Knowing where you will speak and what equipment will be available to you is the third and final element in your working plan. Knowing this information completes the process for creating a preliminary working plan for your speech. The only exception is: planning for the unexpected!

* * *

Although your goal as a speaker is to be so well prepared that nothing will go wrong, anyone who has ever planned an event knows that if something can go wrong, it will. The important thing to remember is that you have considered the three basic elements that will be present during your speech: the audience, the occasion, and the environment. Knowing this information in advance can help you make adjustments if they become necessary on the actual day of your speech. The process of giving a speech is quite complex. It requires more planning than just throwing some ideas on note cards and jumping to the podium. In order to make a success of public speaking, the speaker must consider many circumstantial factors. The working plan is the beginning format for the detailed speech preparation process to come. After all, it is these basic elements that are providing you the opportunity to speak! Unexpected events can cause nervousness and speech anxiety, but if they occur, they can be handled smoothly if you have a well-devised plan.

Speech Anxiety

For many, the nervous anticipation that they experience when they think about speaking to an audience is the worst part of preparing for a speech. Many beginning public speakers, as well as veteran speakers, encounter this rush of nerves. All that is physically required to speak effectively is the skill to connect our thoughts to our mouth—a skill that you already possess. The task you have as a speaker is to find the courage within yourself to use this skill to speak in front of an audience. Research has shown that in the United States alone, speaking in public is one of our greatest fears, preceded only by

Speech anxiety is a common problem, and there are effective ways to overcome it.

death and flying, for some! Why are we afraid? We often ask our students this question and are surprised by some of their answers. Some students fear that they will lose their voice, some are afraid they will trip on their way to the podium, some fear the audience will laugh at them, or think they are stupid. The primary concern that seems to emerge, however, is that the audience will reject their ideas.

Audience members are free to accept or reject whatever is presented to them at any given time. This thought might cause you, as a beginning speaker, to get nervous. After all, no one likes the idea of rejection for any reason. We become nervous and fear that others may not agree with us, or be inclined to listen to our viewpoint. This nervous fear is often referred to as *speech anxiety.* Speech anxiety creates psychological and physical symptoms such as dry mouth, shaking hands, or butterflies in your stomach. Some people get an extreme case of speech anxiety that can cause such intense reactions as sweating, shivering, or red splotches on the skin. It is important for you to know that, in your authors' combined teaching history spanning over forty years, no one has fainted at the podium yet! Public speaking can, however, cause you significant anxiety. The key to controlling this anxiety is understanding what makes you anxious.

What most people really fear as they take the podium the first few times is that they might appear foolish. Remember being called on to read out loud, one of the oldest horrors of childhood? You suffered the pangs of this fear in grade school when you were called on to read or recite an answer. Will I know how to pronounce all of the words? Will I have the right answer? Does my teacher like me? Will my friends tease me about it at recess? Despite whether you did your homework or not, you still were not certain you would get it right, and any public exposure made you sweat. (This is such a common problem that many communication scholars spend much of their time investigating communication apprehension.)

The same is true today, only you are older. Your exposure to the world has taught you that you can be disappointed, you are sensitive, and some people possess the power to hurt you. Now, take a look around the room at your assembled speech class. All of the other students in the room will be required to get up and make speeches—the instructor has this expectation. Are they likely to tease you? Is it feasible that they would wish to hurt you? If they are getting up at the podium, too, wouldn't it be possible that they will treat you as they would wish to be treated? Then, what is the real problem?

The problem is that we are human. We, as human beings, often tend to view the negative aspect of any situation first. The ability to overcome your fears and conquer speech anxiety rests with the ability to overcome the negative and focus on the positive. It is helpful to remember that your audience members are people, too. These people have a responsibility to be audience members and listen to what you have to say. They really do want to hear what you have to say and they want you to succeed. Nevertheless, those thoughts of failure are floating around in your head, while the physical symptoms of speech anxiety begin to manifest. Even if you are able to conquer your thoughts, how can you control your body? What is actually happening inside your body when fear or nervousness strikes?

Symptoms of Speech Anxiety

You need to understand the physical reaction of your body when you are nervous if you want to be able to conquer your speech anxiety. What happens during an attack of nerves? Scientists have determined that *adrenaline,* a hormone produced by the body under stress, flows through your body. This powerful force surges through your body and must find an outlet. This is the same energy that can give you the added boost to run the 440 in 45 seconds. It is "the edge" coaches speak of in athletic competitions, the same energy that allows an athlete to move from last place and win the race. This energy will not just go away; it must be used by the body. Unfortunately, our bodies choose to use adrenaline in several unattractive ways: we sweat, we shake, we turn red, or we have dry mouth. All of these are examples of physical reactions to the source of energy our body recognizes as adrenaline. Even professional speakers suffer from this strange condition, often referring to it as *stage fright.* They describe in great detail how they had to overcome the opening-night jitters but then went on to rave reviews. After all, everyone knows the show must go on!

You know these people, the ones who always seem confident and poised in any speaking situation. They are the ones who enter a room and seem immediately at ease, able to size up the situation and began speaking more confidently. Most of these people did not always behave in this manner. Often they began their speaking careers on as shaky a foundation as yours. They may have felt awkward, fearful, or unprepared, too. What separates them from you is that they have learned to overcome their speech anxiety.

Overcoming Speech Anxiety

There are several suggestions we can make that experienced speakers have used successfully to overcome their speech anxiety. The following five tips can help even the most inexperienced speakers feel more confident in any speaking situation.

1. **Control your fears.** Almost everyone fears the unknown. This is true as you walk to the podium. You fear not knowing how your speech will turn out. This is a perfectly natural reaction in this situation. You need to understand that although you cannot eliminate all of your anxiety, you can control the symptoms it creates.

2. **Think positively.** The mind is very powerful. We often cause situations to happen simply by believing they will happen. Deciding you

can and will deliver an effective speech will take you a long way toward achieving your goal. Think positively and believe that you can get the job done.

3. **Be prepared.** Always pick a topic you are interested in and enthusiastic about. This eliminates doubts you might have if you were speaking about a topic with which you are unfamiliar. Do a complete job of audience analysis before each and every speech. By knowing your audience members' beliefs, opinions, and interests, you can prepare a speech that will keep their attention. You will also be better prepared to anticipate their possible reaction and make adjustments in your presentation if necessary. Re-create the speech environment as much as you can and then practice for your performance. As you practice, imagine yourself walking confidently to the podium and looking at your audience. Enlist a few friends or family members to listen as you practice your speech. Practice it aloud at least three times before your actual presentation. Then practice it again!

4. **Focus on the audience.** Concentrate on your audience to decrease your anxiety. Don't be afraid of making eye contact. Develop rapport and speak directly to them. Don't be afraid of making verbal mistakes. Everyone occasionally mispronounces a word, fails to define a term, or says "um" or "uh" instead of a word. Don't hesitate to be human. It is not necessary to call attention to your nervousness by apologizing, just continue with your speech. Studies show that audiences are much less aware of your mistakes than you think. Concentrating on your fear of making one will only increase the chance that you will actually make a mistake.

5. **Learn from experience.** You aren't the first person to experience speech anxiety. Everyone has had to deal with it at some time or another. Your instructor may not look nervous in front of the class, but that's because he or she has learned how to control the fear. One of us always looked for the trash can before giving a lecture, because she knew she would be sick from nerves when she began to speak! Listen to what your instructors tell you and follow their suggestions. Concentrate on making your introduction flawless—fear is most intense at this time and will dissipate after you get started.

In addition to the five tips given above, it helps if you do not read or memorize your speech. While beginning speakers think this will decrease anxiety, it doesn't. If memory fails (and it usually does), anxiety will increase. Reading your speech leads to a boring speech. Imagine fifty first-graders reciting the pledge of allegiance from memory! Don't forget to make eye contact with your audience. This will allow you to pick up on their feedback. It will also give you encouragement from the nods, smiles, and other signs that your audience will be providing. Use visual aids to add interest and help you present your information. Explaining a chart or picture helps take your mind off your anxiety and gives you another physical outlet for adrenaline.

This woman is relaxed and confident; she has prepared for her speech and is focused on her audience.

Once you have made it through your first speech, you will be more relaxed. You will know you can do it, and your future speeches will be much easier! Speech anxiety is real and expected. It means you care about the outcome of your efforts, and that, in itself, is positive. Despite what you may now believe about your future speaking engagements, you can and will make it through this public speaking class. Think positively, prepare, and practice so you can help yourself overcome your fears. We have a method that we often introduce to our students that seems to help. Let us introduce you to CEM! We have found this method to be invaluable in helping beginning speakers deal with speech anxiety.

The CEM Method

CEM is an acronym that stands for control, eliminate, and mask. Our method uses these three elements to help you *control* your anxiety, *eliminate* your symptoms, and *mask* your nervous behaviors. The first step is to identify what is actually causing your anxiety. Step two is to control, eliminate, or mask the cause. For example, if adrenaline is causing knocking knees or shaking hands, then you would *control* them by channeling this energy into facial expressions, gestures, or dynamic vocal inflections. If your anxiety is caused by feeling unprepared, then you can *eliminate* that fear by researching, organizing, and practicing your speech until you feel comfortable with what you are saying. If your fears simply refuse to go away, you have to *mask* or hide them. One of your authors breaks out in red splotches when she gives a speech. Try as she might, she has been unable to get rid of them. They don't always appear, but when they do, her neck and chest are covered with them. Controlling and eliminating are not options. Therefore, she masks them by wearing a high-neck blouse or turtleneck when she's in a speaking situation that produces them! Now it's your turn to get to know CEM. Use it as a tool to help you overcome your speaking fears.

Strengthen Your Skills

Meet CEM

Purpose: Applying the CEM technique can help you be more at ease with the bogeyman of speech anxiety. Anxiety is a normal reaction to situations in which we don't know what the outcome will be, like giving a speech.

Procedure:

1. Create a list of five nervous symptoms you experience when faced with delivering a speech to a group of people.

2. Investigate each one and decide which ones will need control, elimination, or masking. You may find that you don't have to use all three. You may discover that you can eliminate many by practice and using a positive approach (believing you will do well).

3. Use suggestions from this chapter, talk to others to find out what they do about anxiety, or remember how you overcame it in the past in other situations. The symptoms of nervousness remain the same whenever we are afraid, so if you have been able to overcome anxiety in other situations, such as taking tests or when meeting a new group of people, using those techniques can work when you give a speech.

4. For each of your five symptoms, do the following:
   • Explain what you will do (be specific) for each symptom listed.
   • State what part of CEM you believe will cover the problem.

Conclusion

In the role of speaker, we need to anticipate and plan. If we don't, we often find ourselves unprepared for the situation at hand. Planning your speech decreases the likelihood that you will fail. Butterflies in the stomach, shaking hands, and a general feeling of anxiety are common ailments that novice speakers often experience. They need not spoil your speech. We've introduced you to CEM now it's your turn to put it in action.

Application to Everyday Life

Franklin D. Roosevelt is quoted as saying, "The only thing we have to fear is fear itself." While you may not consider yourself shy, we have all experienced situations in which we allowed fear to keep us from speaking up and expressing our views. Remember that overcoming those fears is courageous. When you disagree with someone, you need to overcome your fear and express your opinion. Planning in all areas of our lives is essential if we are to achieve our goals. So skills learned in public speaking classes are actually life skills.

DISCUSSION QUESTIONS

1. Why is knowing demographic data important for your speech?
2. Why is knowing psychological data important for your speech?
3. Why is it important to consider not only the audience but also the occasion and external environment when you are planning your speech?
4. How does speech anxiety affect you personally?
5. Name three physical symptoms of speech anxiety and supply a possible remedy for each.

KEY WORDS

- adrenaline
- audience analysis
- CEM
- demographic data
- occasion
- psychological data
- speaking environment
- speech anxiety
- stage fright
- working plan

3

Can You Hear Me Now?

Being an
Audience
Member

- We assume that hearing is listening.
- Hearing is a physical act, and is only the first step of the listening process.
- Listening is a psychological act, and consists of a five-step process.
- There are many reasons why we might become distracted and not listen.
- Antilistening behaviors result when we give in to these distractions.
- We engage in these behaviors so often that they become poor habits.
- We can eliminate these habits and improve our listening skills.

Pam is waiting in the conference room for John. Today is their first scheduled meeting to go over the preliminary plans for the annual conference. Pam has developed a checklist of items that need to be addressed in order to make the event function more smoothly. It is now 10:15. She was sure they were supposed to meet at 10:00. Where is he?

John is in the auditorium. He has been checking on the equipment available for speakers. He knows they will have several presentations during the conference, and he has learned from past experience that it is best to check on the equipment well in advance. He remembers attending many sales meetings where the speaker could not be heard in the first few rows, let alone the back row. Where was Pam? He was sure that he mentioned to her on the phone yesterday that he wanted to check the equipment first, before they began their meeting. In fact, he had been making a mental checklist in his head while they were talking. He was sure he had told her he would meet her in the auditorium. Wasn't she listening?

Pam is getting anxious, she has checked her e-mail and her voice mail but has no message from John saying he is running late or cannot attend the meeting. She is trying to remember their conversation on the phone yesterday. She was very busy when he called. She had a client on hold and her assistant was waiting at the door to ask her something. She had misplaced a file and was worried about her daughter's first day of school. She knows she told John she would meet him at 10:00. Wasn't he listening?

In the previous chapter you learned that you have many responsibilities as a speaker. However when you are not speaking you also have responsibilities to fulfill as an audience member. During your public speaking class, you will have the opportunity to be both. There are many preparatory steps to giving a speech, but there are also things you can do to prepare yourself to be a good audience member.

Listening

The most important job that audience members can perform is that of being an attentive listener. Listening is a skill that is very important and yet all too often taken for granted. We assume that if we hear something, we have listened. This is not always true. Hearing is just the first step to listening. It occurs when the reverberation of sound waves in the ear causes a signal to be sent to the brain. In other words, it is the physiological or physical aspect of listening. Just because we *hear* something doesn't mean we *listen* to it; in fact, we hear a large number of things in any given day to which we don't actually listen.

There is more involved in listening than sound waves. In fact listening is a psychological process that involves five steps. Hearing is just the first step in the process. The other four steps are attending, evaluating, retaining, and responding. All five steps must be completed in order for the listening process to have truly occurred. Let's examine what happens at each step so that we can determine ways in which we can become a better audience member.

1. *Hearing* is the first step in the listening process. In this step, sound waves from the atmosphere around us reverberate in our eardrums and send signals to the brain. Our brains receive the signals and begin the process of trying to interpret the audible stimuli. Unless you suffer from hearing loss or some other impairment, this step occurs unconsciously.

2. *Attending* is the second step in the listening process and consists of us trying to pay attention to the sounds we are hearing. We must make a conscious effort to direct our thoughts to the sounds being experienced. In the case of being an audience member, you must pay attention to the words the speaker is using and attempt to understand their meaning.

3. *Evaluating* is the third step in the listening process. In this step we must try to evaluate the speaker's message and attempt to understand what he or she is trying to communicate to us. We will determine if the information is important to us, whether or not it is familiar, or if it matches some prior experience or knowledge that we may have. We often make judgments about a speaker and his or her message in this step, and we sometimes reject or accept the speaker's ideas based on this evaluative process.

4. *Retaining* the information occurs in this step. This is often one of the most difficult steps in the process. We must rely on memory to help us

recall information over a short time span in order to help us continue to understand the information being relayed by the speaker.

5. *Responding* is the final step in the process. If we have been able to complete all four of the preceding steps, then we will provide a response to the speaker that indicates that we have received his or her message. This is the step that constitutes an indication to the speaker that we have attempted to evaluate the message. This is the step that we also know as "feedback," from our study of the communication model in chapter 1.

Now that we have examined the five-step listening process, it is important to realize that the process occurs sequentially. If any of the steps are omitted, listening has not occurred. There are many things that can cause a step to be omitted and skipped. It is these things that distract us and can cause us to be poor listeners and inattentive audience members. You may fool some people into thinking you are listening when you're not, but you won't gain the information that you may need from the conversation or presentation. Although statistics show that for most of the day, people are in situations in which they should listen, only about one in ten people actually do. There is very little risk involved in listening, and the benefits far outweigh the cost of the time spent listening. If listening is so important, why don't we do it more effectively?

Being Motivated to Listen

Most of our communication interactions in any given day are one on one, rather than as an audience member listening to a speaker. However, regardless of the type of interaction in which we are participating, we are often distracted by *external elements.* When these distractions interfere with one of the steps in the listening process, they can cause the entire process to breakdown. Unfortunately it is human nature not to pay attention to information that does not interest or motivate us. Most people need some sensory stimulus to engage them in the listening process.

Research suggests that many of us have one sense that we primarily use to assimilate information. This *sensory mode* is how we comprehend new information. For most of us this primary sense is that of sight. We rely on visual cues to help us make sense of new information. Some people rely on auditory cues, or the things they hear, to digest data, and we all occasionally use our sense of touch to increase our knowledge. What would happen if you, as the speaker, relied strictly on your voice and the words you were speaking to gain the attention of the audience? Would most of your audience pay closer attention to you if they could "see" what you are talking about? The answer is yes.

Audiences also respond to their favorite subjects, or information concerning them personally, but how can you incorporate everyone's personal sensory mode and individual interests into one speech? Speakers must be very clever to construct their message so the audience, as a whole, can relate. The audience's responsibility is to find something in the speaker's message that is personally motivating or interesting. If we can learn how to find that mutual key, we will tend to speak and listen with much more concentration. The problem is that most people have a problem staying focused and concentrating for any length of time. We tend to give in to the distractions around us causing us to display behaviors that indicate we are not listening. In fact, we have a series of slogans that describe these nonlistening behaviors, such as "giving someone the cold shoulder" or "staring off into space." The fact that most people speak at the rate of only 200–250 words per minute, while our brains are capable of processing at least twice that number or more, leaves time for our minds to wander.

Antilistening behaviors result when we give in to distractions. Sometimes we display these behaviors because we do not have any formal training in listening. Some of us are even taught not to listen, primarily through observing how often others tune us out. Just think of all the times you are asked to spend listening in just one day. You listen to teachers, to bosses, to friends, and to family. Because we tend to confuse listening with hearing, we regard listening as a passive activity. We expect it to occur because we have two ears! This expectation causes most of us to be terrible listeners. Although we may have received instruction over the years about how to speak, we very seldom receive any instruction on how to listen. If we have any past training in listening, it was probably focused on antilistening behaviors. For example, Mom says, "We don't listen to that kind of language." Your friend Jane says something hurtful to you and your sister tells you, "Oh, don't pay any attention to her." We are frequently told not to pay attention to what people say. This is not the best method for sharpening your listening skills! Studies have found that improving your listening skills not only increases effective communication but also provides many other benefits such as better grades, better relationships, improved work environments, and increased family harmony. For purposes of this class, sharpening your listening skills can help you to be a better audience member. In order to become a better listener it is important to determine what distractions you are likely to give in to and how you can break this cycle.

Reasons for Poor Listening

We give in to distractions so often that it becomes a habit. *Habits* by definition are any behaviors that we engage in consistently and unconsciously over time. Because of these habits, honing your listening skills can be a difficult process since awareness is the first step in change. Habits are behaviors in which we engage automatically and repeatedly. Therefore we do them without even thinking about them. Tuning out is one of these automatic behav-

It's hard to imagine how this convention planner, surrounded by "to-do list" notes, can listen to her client explaining last-minute changes over the phone. But to be successful at her job, she cannot give in to this distraction!

iors. We are so used to being overloaded with information that we shut down. The first step to overcoming this poor habit and becoming an effective listener is to realize when we are not paying attention and are tuning out. We can then make a conscious effort to get back on track and pay attention.

We are exposed to many messages on a daily basis. We must make decisions as to which information needs our attention. These various bits of information often overload us with messages. This concept, known as *message overload,* is a significant factor in poor listening. We are in situations that require us to listen during most of our waking hours. Our ears and mind are bombarded with messages from people throughout the day. We are expected to listen to friends, family, coworkers, bosses, instructors, and numerous other individuals. We can become distracted by the numerous messages that we receive. When we reach a saturation point in attempting to listen to everything, we often simply tune out. We may do this so often that it becomes a habit, resulting in poor or ineffective communication. Let's discuss some other things that may distract us in the listening process.

We often make *assumptions* about what a speaker might be saying. This, too, can cause us to fail to listen. We may decide that we don't have to listen to what is being said, for many reasons. We may believe that we have heard the information before, that we already know what the speaker is going to say, that the message is insignificant, or that the information is of no concern to us. Sometimes we think that what the speaker is saying is too complicated for us to understand and we would be wasting our time paying attention to the message. We frequently let our perceptions about a speaker's appearance or personality influence our decision to listen. We may not like what the speaker is wearing, or the tone or pitch of the speaker's voice. Although these perceptions may seem unfair, it is often human nature to judge others critically. Sometimes we may fear that the information the speaker is presenting will cause us to feel bad or require us to make a decision. These assumptions divert our attention from the message before we even really know what the speaker is trying to say. We will tune the speaker out, engaging in antilistening behavior once again.

Sometimes we are distracted by noise. We introduced this concept in chapter 1 as any distraction that interferes with the communication process. As an audience member you may be *preoccupied* with other thoughts. This *internal noise* is caused by your own thoughts, your *intrapersonal communication*. Maybe you are worrying about an exam you have to take later in the day, or you are not sure whether you got the job you interviewed for yesterday. When we are preoccupied with our own thoughts, we cannot listen to others. We will often choose, or select, which part of a message we want to listen to and tune everything else out. Most of us are so busy in any given day that we display this habit on a regular basis.

If you have recognized any of your own behaviors in the preceding information then you have taken the first step toward improving your listening skills. If you understand why you tune out, then you can take steps to avoid doing this in the future. This will help you not only improve your listening skills, but also become a more attentive audience member.

Strengthen Your Skills

Not Listening

Purpose: Since awareness is the first step in making any change, and not listening has become a habit, we need to tune in to when we are tuning out! Keeping track of the times you don't listen in an "antilistening" journal is a good way to become aware of your own poor habits.

Procedure:

1. For three days keep track of the times you catch yourself not listening. Include at least five instances per day. This shouldn't be hard!

2. Describe the situation, the topic, and who was speaking.

3. Determine when, and make notes of why, you weren't listening, and what you were doing instead.

4. Be aware of the effect your antilistening behavior has on you, the other person(s), and the situation.

5. After three days, review your journal and try to find any patterns, topics, or people that consistently lead you to tune out.

6. Make a specific plan for improving your listening skills in these situations.

Improving Your Listening Skill

Remember, listening is a skill. Most skills can be learned and practiced. If you want to improve your listening skill and become a more effective listener, the following five suggestions will help you achieve your goal.

1. **Don't expect the speaker to entertain you.** Frequently we believe that it is the speaker's responsibility to make us listen. We think that if the speaker cannot keep our interest, then we don't need to listen. Effective speakers attempt to keep their audiences interested, but that doesn't mean we, as listeners, don't have responsibilities as well. We must mentally prepare to listen to the speaker. Tell yourself that you can stay focused because you want to understand what is being said to you.

2. **Use the speaker's speaking rate to your advantage.** We think faster than most people can speak and this is one reason we may fail to listen. But this can also help us to listen as well. Use the extra time to think about the speaker's words. Review what has been said or take notes to keep yourself on track.

3. **Listen to the message, without the bias.** We often fail to listen because something we see or know about the speaker turns us off. However, information can be learned even from speakers whose images or agendas don't match our expectations, ideas, or opinions. Judge the content of the message, not the speaker, and withhold evaluation until you've listened to the whole message.

4. **Get rid of distractions.** Clear your mind. Put away papers and books that may distract you from listening. Turn off radios, TVs, iPods, phones, or other distracting electronic devices. Try to concentrate on the speaker instead of on your own thoughts. Try not to react emotionally to the message. Filter out noise and focus on the speaker.

The woman in the background is not listening. Although the woman in the foreground appears to be listening, in reality, she is preoccupied, awaiting a text message from a friend about plans for lunch.

In a public speaking situation you have a responsibility to listen when you are part of the audience. You will be providing feedback that will help the speaker to judge the impact that his or her speech is having on you. As a speaker you will need to learn how to "listen" to these messages from your audience. A wrinkled forehead or a shake of the head can suggest that the last point you made was not clear or that your audience is not "buying it." Your listeners may yawn, shift their weight in their seats, lift their feet, or play with the rungs of their chairs—all indications that you, the speaker, have lost them. They may nod in agreement and smile when you state something, showing that you have held their interest. The audience's responses will dictate the course of the speech, perhaps requiring you to rephrase your message, add information for clarification, or reform your conclusion. Your goal as a good speaker is to relay information in such a way that you gain and keep the audience's attention. Your goal as an audience member is to be attentive and listen to the speaker's message.

Conclusion

While we may think of ourselves primarily in the role of speaker in a public speaking situation, much of our time will be spent in the audience. Developing effective listening skills will not only be beneficial for these circumstances but can make all of our communication interactions more enjoyable and productive. We must be aware of things that distract us from listening and take the steps to eliminate these distractions. Otherwise we will engage in poor listening habits and will miss the speaker's message. There are ways that we can keep ourselves from tuning out and improve our listening skills. By using these skills, we can become a good audience member and help the person speaking become a better speaker.

Application to Everyday Life

When people are asked to rank the effectiveness of their daily listening on a scale of 1 (low) through 10 (high), they typically rate themselves at a 7. However, research shows that most would actually rate a 3 or below! When doing the antilistening diary, you probably discovered you weren't as good at listening as you initially thought you were. We can all make improvements by consciously working on being more effective listeners. We guarantee that if you make a concentrated effort to listen you will find that your relationships improve and your grades may also take an upward turn!

DISCUSSION QUESTIONS

1. As a member of the audience, what advice would you give a speaker that would help you be a more attentive listener?
2. As the speaker, what can you do to decrease noise (in all forms) to make it easier for you to have your message attended to by the audience?
3. What does it mean to have a poor listening habit?
4. Name two types of internal noise.
5. What distracts you personally and which of the suggestions that we have made can help you to overcome this distraction?

KEY WORDS

- antilistening behaviors
- assumptions
- attending
- evaluating
- external elements
- habits
- hearing
- intrapersonal communication
- message overload
- preoccupied
- responding
- retaining
- sensory mode

4

It's Not All Talk!

The Speech
Process

- Select the general topic of your speech based on your personal interest.
- Focus your speech by establishing the *specific* topic you will talk about.
- Consider why you are being asked to present the speech.
- Organize your speech so you will know what information you need for support.
- Gather information needed to explain and support your main points.
- Create audio/visual aids to clarify and add interest.
- Create the final notes you will take to the podium.
- Practice your speech several times.
- Consider the vocal and nonvocal elements of your delivery.
- Avoid the common mistakes made by beginning public speakers.

Pam and John have just finished meeting for the third time. They have developed a list of several speakers for the conference. Each speaker will speak about some aspect of the company in general, but each one has been assigned a more specific area to discuss. Most of the speakers are very knowledgeable about the company and their various departments, but John made a point of telling them that many of the other company employees are also very knowledgeable about these details. John told each speaker to be sure to find out any new facts or projects that may be in the works for the company in the next few months and to be sure and share this information with the employees in attendance at the conference.

Pam has told the speakers that the vice president expects them all to create a media presentation to show at the event and they are all expected to use a microphone. Pam and John have scheduled three meetings with the speakers so that they can practice their speeches in the auditorium with the equipment. After all, the company's board of directors will be present at the conference and they don't want any mistakes to occur!

So far we have examined the importance of communication and public speaking in general. We have also discussed what you are required to consider as a speaker, and what you must do when you are a member of the audience. It is now time to take a look at what must be done to create a speech. Many beginning public speaking students believe that preparing a speech is the same as writing a research paper. This is not true! The steps required for preparing material that will be delivered orally differ from those that you might use if you were writing a paper. Although each begins with choosing a topic, the rest of the process differs significantly. In fact we tell our students that about 95 percent of the work they will do to present a speech is in the preparation process. The actual speech will take a very small portion of their time, as most speeches are between three and ten minutes in length. A research paper also requires quite a bit of preparation, but the final document is permanent and can be read over and over again. It is the final document that most students spend the majority of their time correcting, editing, and rewriting. If you are used to writing term papers, the steps we will cover for speech preparation may seem somewhat awkward at first. Nevertheless, once you begin to use them, you will find that they are necessary and effective in helping you deliver an organized and professional speech.

Overview of the Speech Process: Nine Essential Items

Before we begin to look at each aspect of preparing an effective speech, it is useful to look at an overview of the *speech process.* These nine steps incorporate and summarize the concepts, skills, and practices that will be discussed in greater detail in later chapters. Even though we look at these areas separately, they all work together. Seeing the whole picture prior to investigating its individual parts is often a helpful tool in the learning process. This list can also be used as a tool when you are working on your actual speech assignments. Think of this list as a speech in a nutshell . . . the one-minute checklist.

1. **Select a general topic.** Select a *general topic* based on personal interest. Assuming you haven't been given a topic by your boss (or instructor) that limits your choices, pick a topic that interests you. Getting your audience's attention is easier to accomplish when you show enthusiasm in your delivery. This is obviously much easier to do if you already have an interest in the subject about which you are speaking.

2. **Focus your topic.** Next, you must focus, or narrow, your topic. This means you are ready to establish the *specific topic* you will speak about. For example, your general speech topic may be dogs. However there are probably hundreds of different things you could discuss about dogs. You must *narrow* your topic so that it is specific to your interests, the interests

of the audience and the overall purpose of the speech. Failing to give consideration to all three items will greatly decrease your effectiveness.

3. **Consider your specific purpose.** Consider why you are being asked to present the speech. Is it to educate and inform your audience, to convince or persuade them to take some action, or to mark some special occasion or event? Looking at the objective you have in mind (or have been assigned) will help you to form a clear, *specific purpose* in your head of what you want the result of your speech to be. It will also keep you focused on this goal throughout the preparation process.

4. **Organize your speech.** Now it's time to give thought to how you will *organize* your speech. This saves you time when you research your topic, as you will only need to find information for the specific main points you will cover in your speech. Your speech should be organized into three to five main points. These should be apparent if you have done a good job of focusing, as they will address issues you discovered when you completed the audience analysis section of your working plan (chapter 2). If you find yourself with more than five main points, you may need to go back to the focusing step.

5. **Research your topic.** Please note that this is step 5 of the process, not step 2! Don't move from selecting your topic to finding information for your speech. You need to focus your topic so you will know what type of information you need to find; otherwise you will waste time wading through material that does not fit your needs. Remember that there are many sources of information, and you want the most current material you can find to support your main points.

6. **Create** *audio/visual aids.* Beginning public speakers tend to ignore one of the most obvious ways to make a speech more effective. Elements that *show* the audience what you are describing, allow them to *hear* something, or in some other way help them *experience* your words will add to the effectiveness of your speech. Charts, graphs, pictures, PowerPoints, and sound can be used as well as video recordings, CDs, and DVDs. These are all ways of adding dimension and interest to your speech.

7. **Create** *speech notes.* This step is very important and is often ignored by students preparing speeches. Once all of your information has been gathered and you have developed aids for your speech, it is a good idea to create some type of device, either note cards or an outline, which will aid you when delivering your speech to your audience. Many beginning public speakers try to memorize their speeches. This is not the best way to deliver a speech. It is important to have your thoughts written as bullet points in case you forget an idea or stumble during your speech. Creating these notes in advance also gives you the opportunity to use them to practice your speech.

8. **Practice.** Practice makes perfect, right? Well, maybe not perfect, but close. Your goal is to present an effective speech, and *practice* can help you attain this goal. One of the main benefits of practicing your speech, is that it helps you become familiar with what you will say, and how you will say it when you actually present your ideas to your audience. This results in more confidence, and less anxiety, which will greatly enhance your delivery. This step should be done several times. It will make a positive difference.

9. **Deliver your speech.** Many of you will say that this step is the one that you are the most anxious about. If you have completed the other eight steps, much of your work is already done. In this step you will focus on the vocal and nonvocal elements that you will use to deliver your speech out loud. This step occurs when you actually stand in front of the audience and orally present your ideas. You will have eliminated much of the anxiety you feel about standing in front of a group of people and talking because you practiced your speech and are prepared. Remember that speech anxiety is normal and common. Even professional speakers experience it from time to time. You can, and will, be able to deliver your speech!

Mistakes Made by Speakers

In addition to knowing what steps are necessary for delivering an effective speech, it might be useful for you to be aware of several mistakes made by speakers that result in ineffective speeches:

1. failing to focus the speech for the specific audience;
2. attempting to cover too much information;
3. reading the speech word for word;
4. not attributing sources during the speech;
5. failing to use audio/visual aids to help illustrate ideas;
6. not using gestures and avoiding eye contact while speaking;
7. ignoring time constraints.

Obviously, making sure that you have completed all nine steps of the speech preparation process will help you avoid these common mistakes. Although we will cover these issues in more depth in the next few chapters, a few words about each item will give you an idea of why these mistakes should be avoided.

First and foremost is failing to focus your speech for a specific audience. This can easily be avoided if you to take the time to do a proper audience analysis when you develop the working plan for your speech. If you have decided that the specific purpose of your speech is to inform your audience about the

Strengthen Your Skills

Critique Your Instructor

Purpose: Here's your chance to turn the tables on one of your instructors by "grading" their lecture. By critiquing someone else's presentation you can more easily see what you may be leaving out of your own future speeches.

Procedure:

1. Pick one of your instructors and critique his or her lecture one day in class.

2. Refer to the 7 common mistakes above, and note any made by your instructor.

3. Make note of how effective his or her lecture is and why.

type of pet that would best suit their lifestyle, then you must ask questions of your audience to help you determine what that lifestyle actually is. You might need to ask them if they live in the city or the country. You may ask them if they live in an apartment or a house. You may need to know how much time they can devote to the care and training of the pet they choose. By using the information you gain from questioning your audience, you can focus your research, and ultimately your speech, to this *specific* audience. You will be able to tell them that the best pets for people who live in high-rise apartments are smaller pets that can be left indoors for long periods of time, because outdoor areas are not easily accessible. Or you might be able to tell them which pets are better suited to individuals who live in a house with a yard. By specifically tailoring your information to the audience, you can avoid this first mistake.

The second mistake made by beginning speakers is that they try to cover too much information. Again, this is often because they have failed to adequately focus their speech. Sometimes, however, even if your speech is focused to a specific audience, you may still have gathered too much information during the research process. When researching, it is important to carefully consider whether each piece of new information is necessary for a particular audience. Keep in mind your main points and decide if the information you have found supports an idea you are considering. If not, do not use it, no matter how interesting you think it may be! Keep in mind that most speeches have time limits, so you must relay the most important information in the time allotted. Keeping these restraints in mind can help you to avoid making this mistake as well.

The third mistake made by many speakers is that they read their speech to their audience. This results in a boring speech that will most likely put your audience to sleep. Remember our example about the kindergartners who recite the pledge of allegiance after they have memorized it word for word? This is how you will sound to your audience if you attempt to read your

Smiling, relaxed, and confident in her delivery, this young woman is using notes written on cards rather than reading her speech or reciting it from memory.

speech. You will lose the natural inflections of your voice and will probably fall into a monotone. Most people are not natural storytellers and are not able to vary the tone and pitch of their voice to emphasize important points or add interest to the words they are reading. Therefore, you should avoid writing out your speech word for word. We will discuss the correct type of delivery later in the text, but for now pay particular attention to step 7 of the speech process checklist: creating your final speech notes. They should be bullet points or phrases in outline form—not specific statements that you plan to say, written word for word—so that you will not be tempted to read your speech to your audience.

The fourth mistake made by beginning speakers is that they do not attribute their sources in their speeches. In step 5 you have completed the research for your speech. We will cover how this is done and how you can keep track of your sources in the research chapter. For now, keep in mind that you must give credit where credit is due. For example, if you have taken weeks to prepare your speech and deliver it, and then your teacher awards your A to someone else, how would you feel? Not very happy, we imagine! The same is true for other authors or researchers. They have put tremendous effort into researching their areas of expertise. If you are using their ideas to help support one of your own, give them credit. Simply stating in your speech that your information comes from a particular source is easy to do and makes your audience feel comfortable believing what you have to say.

The fifth mistake is one that we tell our students should be avoided at all costs. In fact, we usually require our students to use at least one audio or visual aid for each speech that they deliver. The reason for this is that most people do not learn new information by hearing it alone. Remember, people assimilate new information best through visual means, or by seeing something that relates to the information being presented. This lends support to the idea of creating a visual aid for your audience no matter what that aid might entail. Keep in mind that you must also give thought to the best place or time during your speech to show the audience the aid. Using this element will help your audience incorporate your new ideas into what they may already know or not know about your topic.

The sixth mistake usually occurs because speakers are nervous when they are delivering their speech. This makes them afraid to look at their audience or use their hands. Many speakers try to read their speech, which we have already discussed, and this causes them to look at the podium rather than at their audience. Keep in mind that most face to face communication occurs when people are looking at each other. This is true whether the communication is occurring between you and your boss, or you and your audience. They must be able to see your face and eyes in order to decide if they can believe what you have to say. Avoiding eye contact with your audience would be like avoiding looking at your mom when you were in trouble as a child. She knew when you weren't telling the truth because you would not look at her! This is how your audience will perceive your lack of eye contact, as not telling the truth. This is a mistake to avoid. It is also important to use your hands and face because they add interest while you are speaking. This occurs naturally in most communication interactions. Your audience will expect you to point if you are giving directions, or smile if your information is humorous. If you fail to use gestures and facial expressions at the appropriate time during your speech, your audience will be confused. This may cause them to misinterpret your message. Remember our discussion about this in chapter 1 when we covered the model of communication? Gestures, facial expressions, and eye contact are necessary and important components in all communication, and public speaking should be no different.

The seventh and final mistake to avoid, as a beginning public speaker, is that of ignoring the time limit that has been set for giving your speech. Remember our example about speaking before a dinner engagement? If the dinner is supposed to be served at 7:00 and you have been scheduled to speak for twenty minutes beginning at 6:30, then you are expected to wrap up ten minutes before dinner. This would give you time to return to your seat, as well as give the wait staff time to move about the room and deliver the meals to those in attendance. If you ignore this and speak for forty minutes, dinner is interrupted. Your audience is likely to become irritated and stop listening to you at seven. After all, they are hungry! You will be ineffective as a speaker because your audience will not be able to focus on your message. All they can think about is that dinner will be late, meaning dessert will be late, which means they will get home late, which means they will have to pay the babysitter for another hour! This is just one example of how ignoring a time limit can be a disadvantage. Your goal as a speaker is to make sure your audience gets your intended message. This means they must be completely focused on it at all times. They cannot do that if they are hungry or otherwise mentally occupied.

Conclusion

Now that you've been introduced to the speech-making process, it's time to begin looking at how you can complete each individual step for preparing an effective speech. We know from our experience and research that audiences are more inclined to pay attention to a speech if they can realize some advantage in doing so. If you pay attention to the steps for preparing a speech you can ensure that your speech has personal meaning for your audience.

Application to Everyday Life

Think about a typical day in your life. Picture it in your mind from the moment you wake up until the time you finally fall asleep at night. How many speeches do you give in an average day? Don't be too quick to answer "none." Were you awakened this morning by your mom yelling upstairs to get up? Did you respond with, "It's Saturday and I don't have to go to school or work. I'm sleeping in!"? Did you try to convince her that just because company is coming tonight you shouldn't have to clean your room this morning? That's a persuasive speech. Did you call a friend and discuss last night's party? That's an entertaining speech. What about convincing your two-year-old to take a nap or your boss that you deserve a raise? Did you have to explain to the mechanic what was wrong with your car? All of these are speeches, and you've been making them from the first day you learned how to talk. Making some general decisions early in the planning process can help you to deliver a successful speech. Identifying the type of speech you will give and the style or manner you will use to give it is the next step we will cover.

DISCUSSION QUESTIONS

1. Why is focusing your topic necessary to ensure an effective speech?
2. Why don't you research your speech directly after you choose a topic?

3. Why are audio/visual aids necessary for your speech?

4. Why do you practice your speech several times?

5. Why is each of the "nine preparation steps" essential?

KEY WORDS

- audio/visual aids
- general topic
- organize
- practice
- specific purpose
- specific topic
- speech notes
- speech process

5

When in Rome, Do as the Romans Did!

Types of Speeches

- Early Greek society provides us with the framework for modern-day public speaking.
- Citizens of Greece met in the town square to receive information, to be persuaded, or to celebrate.
- Informative speeches are given with the intent of increasing the audience's knowledge.
- There are five different types of informative speeches: descriptive, demonstration, explanatory, lecture, and report.
- Persuasive speeches attempt to effect a change in attitude, belief, or action.
- There are three categories of persuasive speeches: those that stimulate, those that convince, and those that activate.
- Reinforcement, modeling, and cognitive dissonance are valuable theories that can be applied to persuasion.
- Monroe's Motivated Sequence is an effective tool for organizing your persuasive speech.
- There will be times when a speech is given once in a lifetime, and only on a special occasion.
- Special occasion speeches include, but aren't limited to: introduction, welcome, presentation, acceptance, tribute, nomination, and entertainment.

Several of the conference speakers have telephoned to ask about their presentations. In fact the last caller wanted to know in what order the presentations will be given and how much time each speaker will have to speak. John has realized that although they have determined who the speakers are, they still have much more planning to do. Who should go first?

Pam has also received some calls. She jotted down some notes and has realized that two of the speakers will be giving the employees new information; one sharing information about the new regional policy changes, and the other telling about the new software the company will be using next year. A third speaker will be persuad-

ing employees to sign up for direct deposit. The final speaker will present the company's annual awards. Pam has sketched out the following tentative schedule to show to John:

Speech of Welcome to all Employees	*Who will do this?*
Introduce Vice President, Al Jones	*John*
Keynote Address	*Al Jones*
Introduce Tom Smith, Human Resources	*Pam*
Direct Deposit Program Information	*Tom Smith*
Introduce Jill Jones, Legal Department	*John*
Regional Policy Changes	*Jill Jones*
Introduce Barry Foster	*Pam*
New Company Software	*Barry Foster*
Presentation of Annual Awards	*Who will do this?*
Acceptance of Awards	*12 Honorees*

Pam has realized that each employee accepting an award on behalf of his or her division will probably want and be expected to say a few words after receiving the award. Pam really needs to meet with John. They are going to need to schedule more time for the speakers and find a few more!

The types of speeches you are asked to deliver in a modern-day public speaking class haven't changed much in almost 6,000 years! There is a long history of public speaking in all societies and a well-tested understanding of why speaking effectively is important in these societies.

From Ancient to Modern Times

While it is impossible to pinpoint the date, speaker, or topic of the first speech delivered, we can safely state it predates any written form of communication. Literacy, especially widespread public literacy, is a very recent development in human history. It was the spoken word that spread and preserved information. All societies, tribes, and nations had storytellers whose job was to pass on history and culture. These were honored and respected roles, and were found in ancient India, Africa, China, among the Aztecs, and in other cultures in North and South America. Speaking has always been important to people. The ability to speak clearly, eloquently, and effectively has been recognized for centuries as one of the highly revered characteristics of an educated person. In fact, *The Precepts of Kagemni and Ptah-hotep* (3200–2800 BCE) stresses the importance of public speaking and even gives guidelines for effective communication that are still used today! This document is the oldest book of the Egyptian kingdom and devotes much of its text to the discussion of oral communication, or public speaking. Early Greek, Roman, and medieval cultures devoted much time and study to "rhetoric," which is the theory and practice of public oral communication.

Republics that practice democracy, like the United States, can trace their roots to early Greek society where rhetoric, the art of using words skillfully in speaking, was abundant. Let's think for a moment about the lifestyle these citizens faced. Most communications were done in an open forum. If citizens of Greece were to be informed about a new tax or changes in the barter system, they assembled in the town square for a public forum. If there was a governmental issue being addressed, the citizens again assembled in the town square for a lengthy debate of morals and values relevant to the issue. Even special events such as feasts and holidays were celebrated publicly in this open arena. Citizens were not only encouraged, but also expected, to be present. Since handbills, phones, and the Internet weren't available, any communications were handled orally during these gatherings. Therefore, good citizenship required attending functions in the public forum, and citizens were deemed worthy based on the public speaking skills they displayed there.

These formal gatherings required people to speak for many different reasons. Early Greek society functioned within the framework of a democracy. Citizens may have gathered to receive new "information," whether it was about a new state holiday or a change in taxes. There were times when citizens were called on to debate or vote on a governmental issue. This required citizens to be able to convince others to agree with them; in other words, the art of persuasion was necessary. Finally, citizens were expected to attend special occasions and events held in the town square, once-in-a-lifetime occurrences that required special attention. These early Greek traditions of speaking to inform, speaking to persuade, and speaking for special occasions provide us with the framework for modern-day public speaking. In the United States, teachers of communication still devote considerable effort to teaching methods that support the use of early effective communication techniques within these three categories.

Presenting your speech will depend in large part on your audience. Explaining the effects of tanning to an audience of high school seniors is different from presenting your opinion about how your church committee's budget should be spent, and this is very different from giving a toast at your best friend's wedding. In the first example, you would be providing facts and *information* to your audience. In the second example, you are attempting to get your audience to share your viewpoint through the art of *persuasion*. The final example requires you to speak to your audience at an event designed to celebrate a uniquely *special occasion*. These three examples also represent the three types of speeches in public speaking and are not very different from those of the early Greeks! Let's examine each type of speech a little closer.

Informative Speeches

This type of speech is the one that most of you have heard in the past. The main purpose of the informative speech is the transfer of knowledge from speaker to audience. Since the goal of informative speaking is sharing data, it is important that the speaker know precisely what he or she wants the audience to know when the speech has ended. This requires you, as the speaker, to know your subject in detail.

Informative speeches are given with the intent of increasing the audience's knowledge about a particular subject. A well-prepared and effectively delivered speech of this type has the singular purpose of *increasing* the audience's understanding of a particular topic. For a speech to be informative, you must give audience members material that is not currently known to them and approach the subject in a unique and exciting way. Focusing for your audience is very important for all speeches and should not be forgotten when you prepare a speech to inform. If you look up the word *inform* in the dictionary, you will find: "to enlighten, to bring up to date, and to provide knowledge." An informative speech should do all of these things. It should provide new, enlightening information to members of your audience that brings them up to date on your subject matter while providing them with the overall facts and information that you want them to have. While the general purpose remains the same for all informative speaking situations, the direction and style in which the information is presented can fall into five different speaking categories: descriptive, demonstration, explanatory, lecture, and report.

Descriptive Speeches

The *descriptive speech* is used when the speaker wants to use words to provide a clear picture of a person, place, or thing. In descriptive speaking your purpose is to enlighten your audience by describing your subject in detail. Description is effective only when the language chosen is very specific and graphically detailed. For example, notice the difference in the following two descriptions:

"The sky was shades of blue and pink."

"The sky was cotton-candy blue with various degrees of pink intertwined in an array of swirling hues."

Examples that are understood on the basis of the five senses provide a highly effective mental image for your audience. The descriptive speech works well when you want your audience to have a vivid impression or "picture" of the person, place, or thing about which you are speaking. Examples of descriptive speeches could include: informing the audience about the effects of tanning using examples that describe the process of tanning animal hides, or providing an example of what it is like to be hearing impaired to a hearing audience, or creating an impression of the sensory excitement you felt the first time you viewed the ocean and smelled the salt water! Descriptive speeches are most effective when you enhance your description with audio/visual aids that appeal to your audience's senses.

Demonstration Speeches

The *demonstration speech* attempts to show the steps necessary to take a process from beginning to end. This speech shows how something is done or made, how something works, or how something happens. Your goal in this type of speaking is to present the process in a clear, comprehensive, sequential order that your audience can understand and follow while you are speaking. The most effective demonstrations use many visual aids to show step-by-step (with verbal instructions) how something is done. Actual demonstrations should only be used when you can cover the entire process within the time limit allowed for your speech. Otherwise, you must prepare some steps in advance. The key to a successful demonstration speech is employing carefully worded transitions to lead your audience from one point to another in an orderly fashion.

The most common mistakes made during a demonstration speech are (1) failing to cover all the steps in the process, (2) looking at your visual aids while talking to your audience, and (3) failing to speak while performing the steps. You can avoid these problems through careful outlining and preparation, and by telling your audience what the process is before you actually do all the steps. Examples of speeches that you might "demonstrate" include: how to prepare a budget or balance your checkbook, how to design a Web page, or how to decorate a cake.

Explanatory Speeches

The *explanatory speech* attempts to provide a clear explanation of a complex issue or idea. These speeches work well for subjects that your audience is not very knowledgeable about! For example, you may be a computer whiz in a class full of people who are computer illiterate. In this case, you are an expert who must attempt to explain to your audience the utility of computers, starting with what to do after they turn the computer on to selecting which software program they want to use. It is absolutely essential to use language that your audience can understand. Once you have revised your knowledge into terms that the "average" person can identify, you can follow the guidelines we provided for descriptive speaking. This type of speech can be used for creative, thought-provoking topics as well as complex subjects. Examples of topics that might lend themselves to explanatory speaking are those that explain impressionist painting, "surfing" the Net, nuclear medicine, or our national debt.

Lectures

The *lecture* is a special type of informative speech given by someone with expertise in a particular field. This speech occurs as "instruction" and is often conducted for a large number of "class" members, generally 30 to 150 or more, with the lecturer talking for most of the time period. As you move from class to class in your college experience, be aware of the various techniques used by your own instructors that gain or lose your attention. Some instructors use elaborate diagrams on the board, while others employ PowerPoint presentations or link to a Web site projection. Regardless of the aids employed, the key to lecturing is to be able to keep your audience's attention for a very long period of time and keep them involved in the learning process. This is something that creates quite a challenge—just ask us! We have tried everything from humor, to standing on our heads, to keep the information from becoming dull. We have found that the best way to keep the audience with you as you speak is to incorporate a variety of techniques.

Reports

A *report* is a type of speech normally used in a business setting for a specific purpose or reason. These speeches are usually part of a presentation that may explain the results of data, a survey, a committee project, or a market analysis. Reports are technical in nature and require attention to detail. The information presented must be accurate. Although our immediate vision of this type of speech conjures up a picture of people dozing at a conference table, a report need not be boring. Flip charts, electronic slide shows, colorful handouts, and graphics can enliven the often mundane nature of this type of presentation. Visual aids can provide the impetus necessary to motivate your audience to pay attention to the details of your report.

We have now described the five types of informative speeches: descriptive, demonstration, explanatory, lecture, and report. Remember, in all these speeches, your goal is to educate your audience. The nature of the material, and your audience, will help you to decide which of the five types to use.

Now that we have discussed how to inform our audience, we must remember that this is not the only thing we may need to do as a speaker for an audience. There may be times when you are required to provide inspiration or motivate people to take some action. For example, you may wish for your audience to vote in the next election. For this type of speech you must not only inform your listeners on how they can register to vote, but you must also convince them that it is their responsibility to do so. Motivating your audience in this type of speech requires the effective use of persuasion.

Persuasive Speeches

This type of speech attempts to produce some behavioral response or attitude alteration in your audience members. Persuasive speeches require the speaker to be thorough and convincing in order to persuade the audience to accept his or her viewpoint.

Many people view *persuasion* as the action of a salesperson or con artist. Yet, persuasion is actually an art that requires tremendous skill and, when done ethically, can be a significant factor in positive change. Few of us would ever donate blood if someone had not persuaded us that there is a vital need for it and that it is essentially painless. This type of speech requires getting your audience to think like you. It is accomplished by providing your audience with sound reasons as to why they should accept your point of view.

Persuasion attempts to change attitudes, beliefs, or actions through the use of information. A speech that appeals to an audience is persuasive if it aims to change the audience's thinking, feelings, or opinions. Many of your daily conversations are persuasive, but chances are you have not always been successful in getting others to accept your viewpoint! The skills needed to be persuasive in a conversation are the same as those needed to create a persuasive speech, and therefore must be learned.

Specifically, a **persuasive speech** requires your audience to think critically about the issue being discussed. People who have used persuasive techniques have resolved controversies; activated others to do something; or have motivated others to change their minds. Persuasion can bring about meaningful and important results, such as acquiring funding for AIDS research, creating an international space station, or tearing down the Berlin Wall. Persuasion is a powerful tool that must be used responsibly whether you are preparing to inspire one thousand people or just one. It is a difficult speech to prepare and requires organization and precision. We will devote a bit more time to what constitutes a persuasive speech, but keep in mind it essentially begins as an informative speech and develops into a persuasive speech by adding some essential components. We will begin with an examination of our own beliefs as the building blocks of persuasion.

Belief Systems

To develop a persuasive speech, you first must examine your own opinions or beliefs about the issue in question. Once you are clear about how you personally feel about your topic, you may suggest or propose your idea to your audience. Your belief then becomes a proposition. In persuasive speaking there are three types of propositions. Each proposition accomplishes a different goal.

The first type of proposition is a **proposition of fact,** which argues truth. For example, making the statement that, according to history, a lone assassin shot President John F. Kennedy is a proposition of fact. This is different than suggesting that you believe unions undermine the American work ethic. In this example, you are attempting to argue right or wrong. You are making a **proposition of value.** If you believe that grades should be abolished in college in favor of a pass/fail system, then you are arguing for a course of action or a change in status, thus creating a **proposition of policy.**

Many people believe that propositions of fact are the most persuasive. However propositions of value or policy can be just as persuasive. Be aware that arguing something as fact or policy when it is neither can damage the effectiveness of your speech. Be sure you are clear about your beliefs and how you are proposing them.

No matter which proposition you choose, all persuasive speeches must be logical, ethical, and supported by facts, not opinion. In addition to realizing how you personally feel about an issue, you must also address your audience's beliefs or you will not be able to persuade them to accept your viewpoint.

Appealing to an Audience's Beliefs

In order to persuade audience members that your position is the one they should adopt or believe, you must consider their *needs* and desires in the initial stages of your speech. Basically, human beings have two types of needs: physical and psychological. Physical needs include food, clothing, and shelter. A speaker who suggests a program of buying groceries more economically, lowering fuel bills, or providing a more efficient smoke detector could probably gain immediate audience attention. He or she is speaking about a need all members of the audience can relate to and share.

Psychological needs can be far more difficult to identify, but, as human beings, there are some psychological needs we all share: friends and loved ones are important to most people, as is the need to be a contributing member of society. We also have individual goals and dreams. While the complex personality of each member of the audience cannot be known and may seem to present a challenge too large in scope for any speaker, you can likely identify and address the needs of the group as a whole.

As you look for ways to address needs, you will be faced with many decisions about what might be the best persuasive approach. Should you concentrate on *emotional appeals* (those that pull at our hearts) or *functional* (factual) *appeals* (those that work on our heads)? The answer to this dilemma is to use both. Studies show that emotional appeals are very effective persuasive tools in the short term, yet functional appeals have more long-term results. Therefore, a persuasive speech that grabs audience members by their hearts and gives them facts will optimize results.

Let's say that you wish to persuade your audience to sign a petition that shows they support helping the homeless in America. You could show pictures of homeless people and ask the audience how they would feel if they or their family members lived without a roof over their heads, exposed to adverse weather conditions, having little opportunity to bathe or shower, and never knowing if they will get enough to eat. Once you have gotten the audience's "emotional" attention, you could employ a functional appeal by providing information that shows the relationship of being homeless to poor health and death. You could discuss how living in a warm, dry, safe environment could benefit these individuals. This combination of emotional and functional appeals can convince your audience to take action. You may have your audience asking to help you circulate petitions, not merely sign one!

Learning More about the Audience

Because a persuasive speech is more difficult to prepare than an informative speech, you must present convincing evidence if you want to sway your audience to your viewpoint. Most likely your audience will be committed to their own beliefs and be resistant to yours—at least initially. Most humans are skeptical of change and feel secure in their current patterns of behavior, especially when these patterns have been established on the basis of their morals and values. The longer people have held their established beliefs, the harder it will be for you to persuade them to agree with you. However, there are ways that you can structure information to be persuasive with any audience. Adding some additional questions when you do your audience analysis or doing a second audience analysis will prove invaluable in this situation.

Making assumptions can be dangerous; avoid making any about your audience. Find out as much about your audience and their beliefs as possible. For example, by this point in the speech process, you've had the opportunity to do an audience analysis. If you were giving a persuasive speech in class, you would take the additional time to ask more direct questions pertaining to your specific topic. In addition to the information you may already possess about your audience, it is a good idea to also find out the following information:

1. **What do your audience members already know about your topic?** This will help you decide how much research you need to do on your topic. It's also useful when deciding whether to bring up the arguments against your position, which you need to refute. If they don't know about an argument, don't add fuel to the fire by discussing it. If they do, you'll have to make a defense.

2. **Where did your audience get its information?** Is the audience's information credible? Is it biased? Does the source have emotional appeal or factual appeal? How will you approach negating the source?

3. **What is your audience's position on your topic?** You need to know if audience members' thoughts and opinions are extremely strong, average, or apathetic. Not only do you need to know how they feel about your topic, you need to know the intensity of their convictions. It's one thing if I believe that Habitat for Humanity is a good organization that I would support with a five-dollar donation. It's a much stronger level of involvement if I spend every Saturday for four months helping to build a house. This will help you direct the development of your speech.

4. **What's the audience's emotional reaction to your position?** Are their feelings logical and based in fact? Are there contradictions you can use? For example, if you ask Tracey if she supports a woman's right to choose abortion, she will reply, "Yes, it should remain law." On the other hand, if you ask her how she feels when she thinks about abor-

tion, she will reply, "Sick and sad." It's important to know both reactions if you are going to persuade your audience to adopt your stance.

Once you have completed your fact gathering, you must apply these facts to your original audience analysis. Of course, *audience* is a collective term and within that audience you will have differences. The key to successful persuasion is to attempt to reach out to as many members as you can.

There are three ways that you can structure a speech in order to speak persuasively to an audience. You can structure data to stimulate, convince, or activate your audience. Let's look at each structure in detail.

Structuring Your Speech

A *speech to stimulate* is the easiest of the persuasive speeches because it attempts to strengthen the beliefs already held by your audience. When you give a speech to stimulate, your purpose is to increase the intensity of the attitude and beliefs that members of your audience already possess. The stimulation speech resembles a pep talk. Think of a coach's speech to the team at half-time. If she does her job effectively, the team returns to the game with a renewed sense of direction and an attitude that can strengthen its resolve to win the game. Charities often use this method to get you to donate money. Since many people believe it is "better to give than to receive," their goal is getting you to actually write a check.

Speeches to convince are used to change the audience's mind. The convincing speech attempts to convert the listeners' current way of thinking or behaving to what the speaker is proposing. An example of a convincing speech is to ask the university to use funds that have been allocated for renovating the gym for building a student parking lot instead. It is important to note that you might not change their minds completely in just one speech. You are implying future action overall, but "today" you are only trying to achieve a slight mental shift.

Speeches to activate are used to get your audience to do something. You will ask your audience to take action during your speech. This is the speech that should change behavior. This type of persuasion challenges the audience's normal mode of behavior and offers them an alternative choice. You provide them information that establishes the need for change. For example, a local restaurant now has heart-smart menus and fat-free food choices because customers convinced the restaurant's managers that there was a need for healthier menu choices. These customers not only addressed the problem that these foods were not offered, they made suggestions for specific items that could be offered and how to prepare them. This tactic persuaded the restaurant to take action and actually add the items to the menu.

Logical and Illogical Support

Since persuasive speaking uses the processes of stimulating, convincing, or activating an audience, it is important to make your information consistent. In order to accomplish this you must use logic. There are three useful questions to test the *logic* of your reasoning:

1. Is your evidence current and reputable?
2. Are your sources unbiased?
3. Is the material you are using relevant to your topic and your audience?

If you can answer these three questions affirmatively, then you have presented your audience with clear and consistent evidence that supports your ideas.

Be sure to support your arguments with reliable documentation. The following are examples of ways to build and provide support:

1. **Statistics.** You can use percentages, fractions, or other numbers to substantiate your claim or to show the relationship between two facts. "At year end, 91,612 women were in state or federal prisons—6.6% of all prison inmates."

2. **Narratives.** Relate a documented or historical story. "Long ago, when dinosaurs roamed the earth, . . ."

3. **Anecdotes.** Relate a "personal" story. "The first time I met the person who is now my wife, I had accidentally run into her car."

4. **Analogy.** If two things are alike in certain aspects, they may be alike in other ways. "Christopher Columbus navigated uncharted waters, so too, our astronauts rocket into the unknown, outer space."

5. **Testimony.** Use expert opinion. "We must rally to save the economy! The government supports bailing out the banks before it is too late!"

6. **Sensory evidence.** Use examples that relate to one of the five senses. "We need to stop polluting the air in our neighborhood. Our children shouldn't breathe air that smells like rotten eggs."

7. **Comparing/contrasting.** Show two similar or dissimilar examples of the same process. "Universities practice affirmative action; yet businesses make no effort to hire minorities."

In order to understand clearly what is logical, we will present some examples of what is *not* logical. Therefore, we offer you the most often used *fallacies* (illogical statements). If you make certain that your persuasive arguments *avoid* these, then your arguments are probably logical:

1. **Dicto simpliciter.** Generalization. "Sugar is a source of energy; therefore, the more sugar I eat, the more energy I have."

2. **Hasty generalization.** Too few instances to support a conclusion. "You can't sell your car; I can't sell my car. Therefore, no private owners can sell their cars."

3. **Post hoc.** Cause-effect relationship untrue. "Let's not take Joe with us; every time we take him we get a flat tire."

4. **Contradictory premise.** Premise #1 contradicts premise #2. "[#1] If God can do anything, [#2] can He make a stone so heavy He cannot lift it?"

5. **Ad misericordiam.** Appealing to sympathy. "I've just come from the hospital, so you should believe me."

6. **False analogy.** A comparison of two very different things. "My wife argues like a meat grinder."

7. **Hypothesis.** A statement that assumes fact. "If Al Gore had won the election in 2000, the unemployment rate would not be so high."

8. **Poisoning the well.** Slander or personal attack in an argument. "My opponent is a liar. You'll never be able to believe anything he says."

9. **Loaded question.** Implies an affirmative situation through a question. "Are you still cheating on your taxes?"

10. **Either/or question.** Two extreme choices. "We can continue this administration's deficit-producing policies that bankrupt America, or we can elect a new, honest government by electing Candidate Z."

In order to persuade your audience, you must persuade them that your ideas are valid and supply workable options. Bear in mind that your audience must be carefully and logically led to your point of view with clear and honest evidence. As the previous examples show, illogical support cannot do this for you. Honest evidence is ethical.

Ethics

Ethics, or honesty, in public speaking is important. Ethical speakers are knowledgeable about their topic, convey accurate information, use sound reasoning, and avoid biased information. Ethical speakers do not infringe on the rights of others, and they treat audience members with respect.

Audience members are relying on you to tell them the truth. You are obligated as a speaker to be honest with them and seek the most recent facts and support for your argument. The audience will want more than your opinion when you are talking about controversial issues, such as stem cell research or mental illness. You will need relevant, authoritative sources to support your argument. This means you will have to include more documentation in a persuasive speech than in an informative speech. You must provide your audience with evidence to support your claims. *Evidence* is anything created and substantiated by another person. Evidence should be reliable, current (or, if based on a historical fact, relevant), and unbiased. Quality evidence can produce positive outcomes and can further establish your credibility as a speaker. As you continue the process of structuring your speech, another tool to consider is persuasive technique.

Persuasive Techniques

So much research has been done on persuasion that it's impossible to cover everything. However, the following theories will provide you with an idea of some of the techniques that can be used to your advantage as you structure and organize your persuasive speech.

Reinforcement theory directly relates to your audience's needs. It can be used to convince audience members to believe you or do what you want them to do by pointing out the benefit or reward gained by adopting your viewpoint. Conversely, pointing out the negative effects can show them the disadvantages if they don't adopt your stance.

Modeling theory describes one of the primary ways that we learn. Often our opinions and ideas are modeled on the views and actions of others, particularly those we respect. This theory can be used effectively for persuasion. Providing your audience with examples that have resulted in positive outcomes can motivate them to model your viewpoint. Continuously referring to these positive examples in your speech can be very effective, as most of us learn through repetition. People observe and then model that which is important to them.

Cognitive dissonance theory is based on observations that there is a conscious or cognitive tendency for human beings to decrease dissonance in their lives. Dissonance is an uncomfortable feeling caused by holding two contradictory beliefs simultaneously. This dissonance can be decreased by changing one's attitudes or behaviors so that they are not in conflict with one another. The best way to use this theory as a persuasive tool is to illustrate inconsistency or dissonance in the audience's current stance on your position. Show your listeners how believing as they do is inconsistent with other beliefs they hold dear, or even inconsistent with their goals. This causes dissonance, which creates the need to restore consistency. Used correctly, this can be a powerful persuasive technique.

Another technique that you may utilize is that of *fear.* Not only are human beings motivated by their wants and desires, they are also motivated by the fear of some consequence if they don't do what is asked of them. How often have you studied for an exam because you feared getting a bad grade? In the workplace, not doing your job can result in fear of being fired or demoted. The use of fear can be very effective as a persuasion tool if you are comfortable using this technique. Your appeal to the audience's *"fear factor"* must be factually based and you must provide a way for your audience members to decrease their fear by applying your offered solution. Fear is a powerful emotion, and when tapped effectively, it can provide a strong motivation for affecting your intended goal.

One final technique that you can use to structure your speech is *Monroe's Motivated Sequence.* This five-step organizational pattern originally used for sales was developed by Alan Monroe in the 1930s. This process can be an effective tool for organizing your persuasive speech:

1. **Attention.** Get your audience members' attention and let them know your subject. Prove to the audience that there is a problem, and answer the question "what's in it for me?" (with "me" being an audience member). This will occur in the introduction of your speech.

2. **Need.** Prove to the audience that they need to fix the problem. This starts in your introduction but is developed and supported in the body of your speech.

3. **Satisfaction.** Solve the now-established problem by providing a feasible solution. This occurs in the body of your speech.

4. **Visualization.** Get the members of your audience to see how much better they will feel if they adopt your plan, or how bad they will feel if they don't. This follows the satisfaction step and occurs in the body of your speech.

5. **Action.** This is what you want your audience to do based on your evidence and the appeals you provide. You will develop this step in the body of your speech, immediately before the conclusion, but it should also be included in your conclusion as a *call to action*, a statement that specifically asks your audience to do something.

Strengthen Your Skills

Motivated Sequence

Purpose: This exercise will give you practice in using the Motivated Sequence method for persuasion.

Procedure:

1. Choose a problem you are interested in.
2. Discuss how you would fulfill each of the five Motivated Sequence steps in regard to this problem.

As you can see by our rather lengthy discussion of persuasion, it can be challenging. However, with the proper preparation and organization, you will feel the exhilaration that comes from convincing a room full of people to support you and your ideas.

So far we have discussed informing the members of your audience, and persuading other people to your viewpoint. There is still one category of speaking that we need to discuss. This category revolves around specific events or celebrations. Just as the citizens of Greece had various unique lifetime occurrences, so do we in modern-day society.

Special Occasion Speeches

There are many unique events in our lives that we celebrate. These events often mark special occasions and are generally singular occurrences that require someone to make a small speech, comment, or toast. *Special occasion speeches* require you to work consciously at placing audience members at ease so that they can enjoy themselves. Special occasion speeches are usually very short. Humor may be used, but a speaker need not be a comic to entertain an audience. Speeches given at banquets, weddings, graduation ceremonies, or funerals are given to recognize the importance and uniqueness of the event. The following speeches function primarily as ceremonial or special occasion speeches. For example, speakers are often asked to introduce another speaker, give a speech when they accept an award, or welcome new members at a club initiation. These instances and many others constitute the various types of special occasion speeches.

A speech of introduction is designed to create a connection between someone who is about to speak to an audience and the audience. This speech should briefly tell the audience about the speaker, not disclose everything that the speaker will be saying! It is important to pronounce the speaker's name correctly and stay brief. Do not give the speaker's speech or overly praise him or her. Stay within your time limit, usually two to three minutes, and present only information that is important, such as the reason the audience is there and the purpose of the speech. You are not in the spotlight; that position is reserved for the speaker you are introducing.

A speech given to present an award is a type of special occasion speech.

A welcome speech is designed to introduce your guests to a group and provide a framework for making them feel accepted at an event. It is important to let the people you are welcoming know as much information as possible about the situation and the people present. You should be brief and honest. Make a statement about your hopes that the event will be beneficial for both your guests and the group members present.

The purpose for giving a presentation speech is to give an award (or a prize, gift, or commendation) to another person. You should be brief and to the point, emphasizing the award itself and the person receiving it. You should discuss the history of the award and the reason that it is given. You should then point out the accomplishments of the award recipient and why he or she is receiving the award. Do not overdo and do not under do. Be brief, precise, and to the point.

An acceptance speech is given in response to receiving an award. The purpose of this type of speech is to give honest and brief thanks for the award you have received. You should thank those who helped you to attain the award, but be brief and humble. There is no need to crow about your accomplishments; this would have been taken care of by the speaker who gave the speech of presentation.

A tribute speech should point out the qualities and achievements that a person has attained in his or her lifetime. Tributes occur in many situations such as funerals, birthdays, retirements, weddings, commencements, and keynote addresses. Sometimes a tribute uses humor to "roast" the subject of the speech. When that technique is used, it should be obvious that it is all done lightheartedly and in fun. It is permissible to use humor even in a funeral tribute, or eulogy, but the main goal of this speech is to effectively and sincerely present information about the person's life. Remember to strive for sincerity, no matter what the occasion, while sharing as many details as possible about the honoree. It is helpful to include a statement about what the audience members may have gained from knowing the person to whom the tribute is addressed.

A nomination speech should get attention, be persuasive, emphasize your nominee's qualities and attributes, and be sincere—all in the space of a few short moments. You should be upbeat and enthusiastic so that you will have a positive impact on the audience. After all, you want them to endorse your nominee!

An entertainment speech usually requires the speaker to entertain an audience prior to some other event occurring. The purpose of the gathering will often determine the content of your entertainment speech. For example, if you are gathered to pay tribute to someone at her fiftieth birthday party,

Strengthen Your Skills

Give a Eulogy

Purpose: This exercise gives you an opportunity to practice special occasion speaking.

Procedure:

1. Prepare a three- to five-minute speech that eulogizes the school mascot. If your school doesn't have a mascot, make one up.
2. Present your speech.

your speech might be focused on the humorous elements of aging. Again, be brief, honest, sincere, and don't overdo. Do not expect the audience to be rolling in the aisles with laughter. You are not expected to be Robin Williams, Whoopi Goldberg, or Will Smith!

Whatever the event for which you might be speaking, the major purpose of special occasion speeches is to keep your audience's attention in a light-hearted manner. Humor is generally appropriate and appreciated and is often a major characteristic of special occasion speeches. You are generally provided with advance information that will help you to prepare your speech. You are often more informed about your audience's expectations because you know them personally or because everyone in attendance is there for the same reason. This makes special occasion speeches easier to deliver than informative or persuasive speeches.

Conclusion

Knowing the purpose of your speech can help you prepare and present it. While all speeches will contain information and must attempt to interest and entertain the audience, each of the three types of speeches discussed in this chapter has a unique purpose. Knowing what kind of speech you will give dictates how you will proceed with the speech preparation process and ensures you will deliver an effective speech.

Application to Everyday Life

How often in your day-to-day activities are you in situations in which there is an attempt to persuade you to do something? Your spouse and/or children may want you to run an errand for them. Your parents may need you to clean up your room, mow the lawn, or fix dinner. How many hours a day do you spend watching TV, listening to the radio, surfing the Internet, or reading magazines/newspapers? All of these forms of media contain advertisements that are pure persuasion. How often do you attempt to get others to do what you want? How often do you get them to do it? If your requests are going unanswered or people are arguing with you about what you want, you will find that the same skills required to give an effective persuasive speech will help you to be more persuasive in everyday life. Furthermore, these skills can make you a better, less gullible consumer of the media and others' attempts to persuade you to do something.

DISCUSSION QUESTIONS

1. What are the three main categories of speeches?
2. What is a descriptive speech? How is it different from a demonstration speech?
3. What are the three types of persuasive speeches? How do they differ from each other?
4. Why are both emotional and functional appeals necessary for effective persuasion?
5. What does *ethical* mean? Why is it essential to persuasion?
6. What is the main reason for a special occasion speech? What are some characteristics that all special occasion speeches should have?

KEY WORDS

- call to action
- cognitive dissonance theory
- demonstration speech
- descriptive speech
- emotional appeals
- ethics
- evidence
- explanatory speech
- fallacies
- fear
- functional appeals
- informative speech
- lecture
- logic
- modeling theory
- Monroe's Motivational Sequence
- needs
- persuasive speech
- proposition of fact
- proposition of policy
- proposition of value
- reinforcement theory
- report
- special occasion speech
- speech to activate
- speech to convince
- speech to stimulate

6

Eenie, Meenie, Minie, Mo? No!

How to Begin
a Speech

Chapter Highlights

- The first thing to consider when choosing a topic is you.
- Brainstorming, hitchhiking, and general conversation are good techniques for choosing a topic.
- Our daily routine can also provide us with speech topics.
- The Internet can provide numerous topics as well.
- Focusing is the process of narrowing your speech topic to reflect what effect it will have on the target audience.
- Forming a specific purpose statement is done after the focusing process
- A specific purpose statement is a simple complete sentence that states the audience's expected response at the conclusion of the speech.
- This statement must be worded clearly and concisely.

John has set up a meeting with Tom in Human Resources. Tom will be persuading employees to sign up for direct deposit during the conference. Tom was not sure what to say. He has worked for five years in the department and has a degree in employee relations. He is certainly qualified to present the information. He has a thorough knowledge of the program at his division, but he is not sure how much the employees at the other division know about the program or how many currently participate. He does not know if he is expected to actually sign the employees up for direct deposit during the conference or give them packets to take with them. He has just jotted down some questions to ask John.

Will all of the divisions and their employees be present?

Will he be the only Human Resources employee available to help with the forms?

Are all employees companywide eligible to participate in the program?

Does he have access to their personal information to facilitate the sign-up?

Tom must stop for a moment to attend another meeting, but he plans on finishing his list of questions later. After all, direct deposit is a very general topic. How will he narrow it to be more specific in order to provide the information that employees of this company actually need?

Choosing a topic should be the first step toward developing a speech. However, to make that topic turn into an *effective* speech you'll have to consider yourself, your audience, and your speaking environment. The result of this process will be a specific purpose statement that clearly defines your goal.

Choosing Your Topic

The first step to presenting a great speech is to choose a topic. What will you speak about? While this should be the easiest and least time-consuming of all the steps you will take to prepare a speech, novice speakers often find this a difficult task.

The first thing to consider when choosing a topic is you! What do you know that might be interesting to someone else? Experiences have happened to you in the past and continue to happen to you every day: fascinating, funny, frightening events occur that could make excellent topics for speeches. The major objective at this point is to decide what you can talk about that won't require mountains of research to support. You may believe that you are a boring person, to whom nothing ever happens. This is just not true! You could talk about a recent problem you had in school, a family crisis that you are facing, a new hobby, or your job. Any of these subjects would make a very good three- to five-minute speech. Additionally, these topics are all about you, a subject that most audiences will find fascinating. After all, humans are very curious creatures, especially when their curiosity involves finding out about other humans. Remember your audience members will enjoy relating their experiences to your own as well. When we share personal information in this fashion, we are placing ourselves in a larger context, tying our experiences to those of our audience. Through this sharing of experiences, we become connected personally to our listeners and will be speaking about experiences they can readily understand.

How can I, Mary, turn my altercation with the manager of a local discount store into a speech? I might talk about the rude clerks and employees we have all encountered. I might speak about the pressure the employee faces when having to deal with an irate customer for whom he is totally unprepared. I might discuss, in involved and humorous detail, how I tried to return a defective bedspread to the store. I insisted I had purchased it there; only to find out I had purchased it at the discount store down the street. After all, the store name was printed right on the receipt! This speech does not have to be looked up or researched, it really happened to me! But with a little research effort I could easily add to the content by discussing various store return policies and procedures.

Determine What You Know

The easiest starting place for generating a *speech topic* is to stop for a moment and think about everything that you personally know. What are some hobbies you have had in the past? What sports did you play in high school? What are you currently involved in outside the classroom? Do you have any particular interests or concerns about your life or your health? Do you find your job interesting, fulfilling, or time-consuming? What is your experience of college? Let's explore these ideas further with some examples.

Suppose you are concerned about how much time you are spending outside in the sun. After all, you have heard the warnings about skin cancer. You know that exposure to the sun at an early age can cause problems later in life. After talking with your doctor, you now wear sunscreen if you are in the sun for prolonged periods, and you also wear a hat when you go fishing. As you continue to explore this experience, you must keep in mind that your audience is composed of people who probably have shared a similar experience. This is to your advantage because it allows you to speak to them about something they can easily relate to. However, you must not bore them with information that they might already possess. Finding some detail or fact that they might not be aware of is important. For example, you might mention that leather is derived from exposing skin to intense chemical heating processes. Not a pretty picture when applied to our own skin! You could explain what to look for in sun protection products. You could explain the concept of ultraviolet light, harmful rays, and SPF. The goal here is to start with something familiar that your audience can grasp and then expand your coverage to include information that is unique. In fact, linking new ideas to those already known by your audience is a very effective technique.

Determine What You Don't Know

To find "unique" information about a subject, you must be willing to explore and be critical with yourself to decide what you don't know. Although you have some previous individual experience with various subjects (a good starting point), there are details and points about each that could be added to your knowledge. For example, we have all read and studied about the Declaration of Independence. Most people know that it was written in Philadelphia. What you might not know is that it was written during the hottest summer on record! How would you behave if you had to sit in a stuffy, un-air-conditioned hall, in the elaborate and hot clothing of the day, with people who bathed once a week at best, debating the future of your nation? This tidbit, added to your speech on the importance of democracy in society, might be just the unique information you need to keep your audience interested.

Most people know what a raccoon looks like. Some people wear hats with a raccoon tail attached. Did you know that a raccoon uses its "hands" to cause all kinds of mischief and will wash each individual morsel of food before eating it? This is another example of how you can find information to add to your own personal knowledge and interest your audience as well.

You must be willing to research the possibilities of everything you don't know to make your speech interesting! Research is also important to make sure facts are substantiated. You will be spending a lot of time with your topic, so pick something you are really interested in. Don't choose a topic just because you think you can easily find the research material.

By beginning with a topic that interests *you*, your research will become exciting as you find out all the unusual facts about your topic. Your research will be easier and more efficient if you have interest in your subject, and you will be motivated to stick to your topic. Consider this the cardinal rule of speech making: When possible, *pick a topic you are interested in!*

Ways to Find Topics

Brainstorming

One easy technique for generating speech topics involves writing down ideas "off the top of your head." This process is called *brainstorming.* The best way to brainstorm is to sit and quickly list ideas as they occur to you, until you collect many ideas. Problem-solving groups in corporations often use this method when they are looking for solutions to unusual problems or addressing challenging concerns. The key to brainstorming is to suspend judgment while ideas are generated.

A large discount store has always had a no-smoking policy for its customers. However, employees were allowed to smoke in the cafeteria and lunchroom on breaks and during their lunch period. Once the store initiated a storewide no-smoking policy, which applied to both customers and employees, workers were no longer able to smoke in the building. Employees began to hang out in large groups outside the building to smoke during their breaks. Company management felt this looked very unprofessional. Reports showed that customers believed they would not be able to get help inside the store because all of the employees were outside smoking! Therefore, customers were choosing to shop elsewhere. Regardless of whether these customers' perceptions were true, the store now had a "perceived" problem.

To find a solution to this problem, the store had to suspend all judgment until a large number of possibilities was generated. They formed a committee of people to find a solution to the problem. It did not matter whether the committee members were smokers or nonsmokers. The key was to list as many possible solutions as they could. Some suggestions included: banning smoking on company property, hiring only nonsmokers, no breaks, no lunch, and so forth. As you can see, brainstorming does not always produce feasible (or legal) solutions! However, the company eventually came up with the plan of providing a large outdoor seating area, furnished nicely with tables, chairs, flowers, and ashtrays. Employees were happy, and customers perceived the company as wonderful for giving its employees such a pleasant break area.

Also, customers no longer negatively perceived the employees as unavailable. So, generating a list of possible solutions and then choosing the best one for an individual situation solved a "perceived" problem.

Another technique to aid you in the brainstorming process is to use *hitch-hiking.* Hitchhiking is the process of building off of other topics/subjects you have already listed. Suppose as you are brainstorming you write down "fast food." That might trigger several related topics such as McDonald's, Burger King, Pizza Hut, pizza, hamburgers, and so forth. That's hitchhiking.

Strengthen Your Skills

Brainstorm Topics

Purpose: The purpose of this exercise is to take you through the process of choosing possible topics for speeches by brainstorming.

Procedure:

1. Your instructor will divide the class into small groups of about four or five people each.

2. Each group should appoint a record keeper. If someone in the group takes shorthand or writes quickly, that's your person.

3. For ten minutes, group members will throw out possible topics while the record keeper writes them down. Keep the following rules in mind:

   a. Simply list ideas, don't judge them.

   b. Hitchhike off others' ideas. If one person says "music," add ideas that stem off that, like "rock," "hip-hop," "alternative," "country," etc.

   c. Remember that your purpose is to compile as many topics as you can.

4. At the end of ten minutes, stop and review your topics. Could any of these be a speech topic? How many are you interested in personally?

General Conversation

Another excellent method for generating topics is *general conversation.* There are several times throughout any given day that you will find yourself sitting with friends and acquaintances, having a conversation. You may be waiting for a class to begin or chatting over lunch at McDonald's. You might be sitting at your computer and receive an instant message from someone on your buddy list. You share opinions and concerns while you chat. Someone may be concerned about his or her grades; another may be having financial difficulties, while you may be worried about getting the flu! Each of these seemingly minor subjects could produce a speech topic. For example, concerns about grades could lead to a speech on how to study, various testing methods, course selection, course requirements, financial aid, choosing a college, deciding on a career, and so on. These ideas, although started in general conversation, can be brainstormed or hitchhiked into an enormous list of possible speech topics!

Other Sources

Our daily routine can also provide us with speech topics. Your local newspaper and various magazines that you read offer a wealth of useful, interesting, and most importantly, current information. Your browser home page usually includes headlines and stories of interest. These are often the best sources for up-to-date facts on issues. With the emergence of affordable satellite dishes and inexpensive cable services, your television can also offer you many ideas. There are several learning channels, animal-oriented stations, and reality adventure series, among many others, that can give you interesting facts to begin or support your speech. Digital recording makes it simple to record these potential sources for perusal later. Also, don't forget you! Your personal daily routine can provide you with a viable speech topic. We take much of our daily routine for granted. For example, brushing our teeth is something most of us do at least once per day. This topic alone can provide several speech topics: good oral hygiene, tooth decay, gum disease, and dentures, to name a few! These are topics oriented to your own life and can be easily shared with your audience. In addition, familiar quotations or sayings can serve as good topics for icebreaker speeches. On the following page, we have provided an exercise using this idea.

The Internet

Finally, don't forget the Internet. (See chapter 8 for a more detailed discussion of the Internet.) Just one page of a single site will provide you with a multitude of possible topics. Even those annoying pop-up ads can have a use for *you* rather than the advertiser. Another idea is to use your favorite search engine (see chapter 8) to search general topics. The result should give you lots of ideas without even linking to the sources. For example, a search for *television* will result in thousands of possible topics, from a biography of Milton Berle to television's effect on our culture. Don't get bogged down, pick a single topic and get started!

Focusing Your Topic

Once you've decided on a general topic for your speech, it's time to fine-tune that topic by focusing. *Focusing* is the process of *narrowing* your speech to reflect what effect it will have on the target audience. Don't forget, some of the most common mistakes made by speakers are:

1. Failing to create a speech that is focused for a target audience
2. Being poorly prepared, or not adequately researching the topic
3. Attempting to cover too much information in the time allotted
4. Failing to maintain eye contact during speech delivery
5. Relaying information that is dull or boring

Note that all of the above problems, except number 4, can be avoided by focusing your topic. If you want to be a successful speaker, you need to learn how to

Strengthen Your Skills

The One-Proposition Speech

Purpose: This exercise gives you practice in focusing on one central idea. You will create a short speech that explains one proposition and illustrates it in a variety of ways.

Procedure:

1. Choose one of the following parables as your speech topic:
   Don't cry over spilt milk.
   The grass is always greener on the other side of the fence.
   If at first you don't succeed, try, try again.
   A stitch in time saves nine.
   An ounce of prevention is worth a pound of cure.
   Early to bed, early to rise, makes a man healthy, wealthy, and wise.
   Blood is thicker than water.
   A penny saved is a penny earned.
   Walk softly and carry a big stick.
   No man is an island.
   If the shoe fits, wear it.
   Man does not live by bread alone.
   The die is cast.
   The early bird catches the worm.
   Beauty is only skin deep.
   Nice guys finish last.
   No news is good news.
   It's not if you win or lose, but how you play the game.
   It's not over 'til it's over.

2. Use any type of speech (informative, persuasive, or special occasion) to tell your audience what the statement means to you in your own words. Try to avoid the actual statement if possible.

3. Present your speech.

A successful speaker uses his or her own interests as a factor in selecting a topic and delivering a speech.

properly focus your speech. This is one of the most important elements of an effective speech, but it's also one of the steps beginning speakers fail to do thoroughly. Remember that the time and effort you put into this simple process will decrease the amount of time you spend on research later and lead to a much better speech in the end. The focusing process is done in three easy steps; consider the speaker, consider the audience, and consider the occasion.

Consider the Speaker

The first step in narrowing considers you as the speaker. Ask yourself the following three questions:

- What *interests* me about this topic?
- What is the *purpose* of this speech?
- What *knowledge* do I have about this topic?

Interest

A successful speaker always uses his or her own *interests* to help decide what message will be sent. Even if the topic is assigned in some way, like a business report you've been asked to prepare, it will be much more effective if you show enthusiasm and enjoyment for the topic.

Let's suppose you have chosen the author Anne Rice as your general topic. In this part of the focusing process you should narrow that topic so that it reflects a clearer statement of why Anne Rice is interesting to you. Will you talk about her books or her personal life? If you decide it's her books, which genre will it be—vampires, witches, her erotic works, or her series on Christ? Which do you personally find most interesting?

Purpose

Next you must consider the reason you are presenting the speech. Do you want to persuade your audience to read a series of her books? Do you want to inform them about her personal depression and bout with alcoholism after the death of her child or her return to religion after decades of being an atheist? What *purpose* will this speech fill? One way to determine this is to make a list of objectives. For the Anne Rice speech this list may include learning about the Vampire Lestat, reading all the various vampire books, or believing that personal adversities can be overcome. At this stage you may have several ideas, and that's fine.

Knowledge

The last step is to consider what *knowledge* you have about your topic. Even though you are interested in the topic, there are probably some areas that you have more knowledge about than others. Your speech should be about the area in which you have the most information. You'll most likely need to enhance the information you already have by doing research, but having a good basic knowledge of your topic not only gives you a starting point, it also means you'll spend less time searching for data and more time preparing an effective speech. Using the Anne Rice example once more, if you know little about her personal life but have read all the vampire books, your choice should be obvious, go with the books!

At the end of this process you will have a better idea of what your topic will be. In fact, you probably will have several possible speech topics. The next step in focusing will whittle down all these possibilities by considering the most important element, your audience.

Consider the Audience

Your audience is the *reason* you are speaking. You may think you are speaking because of requirements from your boss or your teacher. You may think you are giving a speech for a grade or to follow orders. While these are certainly common elements of some speaking situations, seeing them as your main purpose won't result in an effective speech. Many of us might think we would prefer not to have an audience for our speech because it would decrease our anxiety, but what purpose would that really serve? Speaking without an audience might be an exercise in self-indulgence, but it certainly wouldn't be a speech. A speech requires a speaker *and* an audience. You are only one part of the equation, and you've already considered yourself. Your

Audience analysis for a commencement speech might not be time-consuming, but the speaker still needs to creatively focus on the audience's purpose for listening to the speech, so that it will resonate with all members of the audience—even the graduates' family members.

audience is the other part of the equation. You need to consider them too when focusing your topic. Finding the answers to these questions can help:

- How can I make this topic of *interest* to my audience?
- What is my audience's *purpose* in listening to this topic?
- What does my audience already *know* about my topic?

This part of the narrowing process relies heavily on your audience analysis (chapter 2). The importance of your audience analysis must not be ignored. We've found that many beginning speakers tend to do only a surface analysis, if any at all. Earlier in this text you learned how-to do an audience analysis. Now it's time to apply what you found out!

Interest

A topic that is of no *interest* to your audience will result in a doomed speech. You need to make sure your speech topic is interesting to them. In order to do this, you will have to consider your audience's interests, but also much more. Just as you needed to know what made your topic interesting to you, you need to know the same thing about your audience. What aspects of your topic will your audience find most interesting? You can't cover everything; so you need to choose carefully based on those interests that you and your audience share. Remember you are talking to a *specific* group of people. You may be able to use the same general topic for different groups, but it must be individually tailored to the specific interest of each group.

Even after beginning speakers choose a topic, the next stumbling block they often come up against is the belief that what they are interested in will bore others. How can you gain and maintain attention? What interests do you and your audience share in regard to your topic? Consider the following true example of how you might approach this problem.

Mark was enrolled in a public speaking class. There were three men and fifteen women in the class, which met on Monday nights during the fall semester. Mark loved football and wanted to do his informative speech on some aspect of that topic. However he was well aware that the majority of the class wasn't interested in football. While he bemoaned the fact that he was missing the televised games on Monday nights because of class, he had heard many of the women saying they were glad to attend class and let the men in their homes have the TV on Monday evenings. How in the world would he focus this topic so that it worked for his audience and himself? There was a solution, and it worked beautifully! Mark decided to do his speech on the hand signals the officials use to call a play. Instead of just explaining them in the context of a football game, he took the interests of his audience into account. He described a couple out on a first date. Every time the guy made a move that corresponded to a hand signal (like fumbling, unnecessary roughness, or touchdown), he had a female member of the class demonstrate the signal in his speech. His audience paid attention, enjoyed themselves, and learned more about football from his speech.

Purpose

Not only do you have to consider your audience's interest in your topic, you also need to make sure your topic relates to the reason your audience has gathered. What is their *purpose* for listening? Why should these people listen to *you*? What will they learn or be able to do at the end of your speech? What needs will your speech fulfill? Will they have a new easy-to-make recipe, have a better understanding of how the stock market affects them, or be better informed voters? Will they save money, be healthier, or be safer in their homes?

Discovering your audiences' reason for being present helps you focus your speech. For example, you would probably assume that most of your classmates are enrolled in this class to fulfill a requirement for graduation, with the greater goal being a degree, certification, or promotion at work. While that would be a fairly accurate assumption, what other reasons could they have? Are they there to socialize, or get out of the house while the kids are at school? Are they there to prove to someone that they are intelligent? Finding out other possible reasons may help you relate your speech topic to your audiences' actual purpose for listening to you.

Incorporating these reasons in your speech can help your audience achieve the specific purpose you have for them at the end of your speech.

Knowledge

The audience's knowledge level should also be considered as part of the focusing process. While some people may politely sit and listen to a speech about something they already know, this is the exception rather than the rule. Most, while not "voting with their feet" and walking out on you, will tune out. They will quit listening, and as mentioned before, a speaker without an audience can't deliver an effective speech. You need to know what they know. Is their knowledge basic or does a significant part of your audience have advanced knowledge about your topic? Giving a speech on the basics is good if your audience knows very little (or has misconceptions) about the topic. Giving this same speech to a group that already knows the basics is poor focusing. You want to provide your audience with new information, fascinating data, and new ways of thinking about your topic. Of course, you probably won't have an audience in which all members have the same level of knowledge. You'll have to aim for the middle ground, yet not ignore the lower and upper knowledge levels.

Adapting your topic to a specific audience is probably the most important part of the focusing process. Doing a thorough audience analysis, before attempting this step, will make this process easier and more effective.

Consider the Occasion

Once you've considered the speaker and the audience, the last part of the focusing process considers the occasion for which you are speaking. To understand the speaking occasion, ask yourself the following questions:

1. What *event* am I speaking at?
2. What is the *physical environment* I will be speaking in?
3. What is the *time factor* for my speech?

Supplying answers to the above questions will complete the focusing process and prepare you for the next step in developing an effective speech.

Event

What is the *event* for which you are preparing your speech? Is it a wedding, athletic banquet, or business meeting? While the same topic may be used in several different situations, the focus of that topic may change depending upon the event at which you will speak. The focus of your topic would be completely different for a speech given at a church function than for a speech at the local Harley club. If your topic was persuading people to vote for a particular candidate, you might focus on the candidate's values or morals when speaking at a church function. In your speech to the Harley club, you might emphasize your candidate's stance on issues of interest to them (e.g., helmet laws, highway safety, tax advantages for nonprofit organizations, etc.). You might use humor in both speeches but change the amount and type used. You might choose different language or words for the church group as compared to the motorcycle club. Think about the event and make sure you focus your topic appropriately.

Physical Environment

Knowing the *physical environment* in which you will be speaking and what equipment you will have available to you is also important. If you are speaking in a fifteen-hundred–seat auditorium, you will need different equipment than if you were speaking in a board room. Will you need a microphone to be heard? Do you have the equipment available to deliver a multimedia presentation, or will handouts be necessary? Will the audience members be close enough to you to see small photographs, or will they have to be scanned and projected onto a large screen? These are just some of the factors you need to consider about the physical location where you are speaking.

Time Factor

The last step when considering the speech occasion is the *time factor*. You've considered the event, and the physical environment for the occasion you will be speaking at, but will your topic fit within your allotted time? In many ways, this last step is the most difficult. All speeches have time limits. Time limits are important. Former President Clinton is an experienced speaker and is considered by many people to be very eloquent. He could enchant his audience. However, he was never able to speak in the allotted time frame. Traditionally, the president speaks about an hour to Congress. President Clinton's speeches typically lasted two hours. He could not stay focused, often rambling and deviating from his script. Since his speech did not stay focused, he was not effective with Congress or the American people watching him on TV. Know what your parameters are and stay within them. Failure to focus for the time limit can have several unpleasant results.

Trying to cover too many points in your speech, or not covering enough can leave the audience feeling cheated or confused. Further, if there are events planned in addition to your speech, a speech that takes more than or less than the allotted time can interfere with the schedule. Let's say you have been asked to speak for thirty minutes and your speech is an hour. Whatever follows your speech, be it another speaker, dinner, or the audience's dismissal to do other things, is disrupted if your speech runs past the allotted time. If dinner is served late, the hungry audience could be crabby—certainly not an ideal situation! Know what your time limit is and make sure your speech fits within your time frame. The focusing process is an important part of preparing an effective speech. It is a necessary process to achieve your goals. No step should be skipped.

Strengthen Your Skills

Focusing Your Topic

Purpose: The purpose of this activity is to give you practice in how to focus a topic.

Procedure:

1. Make a list of five general topics that consider you as the speaker. Choose topics that you are interested in, that you know something about, and that would serve the general purpose of either informing or persuading your audience.

2. Now consider your audience. This could be your classmates, people you work with, or the membership of an organization with which you are familiar. It doesn't matter what group you pick, just make sure you have a specific audience in mind. For each of the topics you listed in number 1, decide what changes need to be made to make it interesting to your chosen audience by considering their knowledge and purpose for listening.

3. Now consider an event, physical environment, and time factor (say 5–7 minutes) for each topic.

The result of completing this process will allow you to create a clear statement that takes into consideration you, your audience, and the occasion. If you can't state your speech topic clearly in one sentence, you haven't focused effectively. This sentence is known as a specific purpose statement, and will be the guiding point for the rest of the speech preparation steps.

Forming a Specific Purpose Statement

A *specific purpose statement* is a single sentence that states the response you hope to elicit from the audience. This statement is developed from the focusing process. In one simple sentence, you will state the intent and desired goal of your entire speech. There are a few guidelines to follow when creating a specific purpose statement.

Guidelines

A specific purpose statement reflects the speaker's interests, knowledge, and purpose, while taking into account the audience's interests, knowledge, and purpose. This statement should follow three guidelines:

1. It must be written as a simple *complete sentence.*
2. It must be worded *clearly* and *concisely.*
3. It must state the *expected audience response.*

The first guideline is: a *specific purpose must be written as a simple complete sentence.* In this case, a complete sentence means that you must include one, and only one, subject in your statement. "The audience will be able to make a banana split" is a simple sentence with one subject and one verb. "The audience will be able to make a banana split and I will show them the best way to eat it" is a compound sentence with two subjects and two verbs and, therefore, doesn't meet the requirements of a specific purpose statement. This doesn't mean that you cannot cover more than one idea in your speech (depending, of course, on the time limit). However, it does require you to be specific about the *ultimate* goal of your speech. That goal should be worded as one subject. You may discuss several ideas to reach that goal, but ultimately your goal is one, and only one, subject.

The subject of all specific purpose statements will be the audience. It will be the audience that is doing, knowing, or being persuaded in the sentence. Example: "The audience will know how to hang wallpaper." The verb is "will know." Who or what will know? The audience will know. By finding the verb in the statement and asking, "Who or what is doing the action of the verb?" you will discover what the subject is (it should be the audience) and be assured that you have a complete and correct sentence.

The second guideline: *it must be worded clearly and concisely,* means that your specific purpose should be easily read and understood. You should make your statement as short as possible and use words that say *exactly how you want the audience to react.* "The audience will know about the Federal Reserve System" is not worded clearly and concisely. It is written in the proper form, but it does not state precisely what the speaker wants from his audience. What, specifically, about the Federal Reserve System does he want his audience to know? Should the audience know how or why it was formed, its purpose, what effect it has on our economy, or why it should be changed or abolished?

A clear, specific purpose statement for an informative speech on this topic might be, "The audience will know why the Federal Reserve System was founded." A specific purpose for a persuasive speech might be, "The audience will be convinced that the Federal Reserve System should be abolished."

The third guideline: *a specific purpose states the expected audience response*, means that it should address what you want your audience to know or do at the completion of your speech. "I will tell my audience to donate blood to the Red Cross" is not a proper specific purpose statement for a persuasive speech because it does not include a response from the audience. It states what the speaker will do, but it does not state what the audience will do. "The audience will donate blood during the next bloodmobile drive," states exactly what the audience will do. This may seem nitpicky, but there is an important reason for doing this.

When you state you are going to inform, tell, motivate, persuade, or convince your audience, you are referring to what you, as the speaker, will be doing in your speech. Obviously, the purpose in giving any speech is focusing initially on *how* you will persuade, entertain, or inform your specific audience. It is equally important that you state what you want from your audience at the conclusion of your speech. Writing a specific purpose statement forces you to consider how the audience can be motivated to achieve the goal you have established. After all, your purpose in giving a speech should be to reach your audience. Otherwise you might as well be speaking to an empty room, or not speaking at all.

Examples

Remember that the subject of a specific purpose statement will be your audience; the audience will perform the action or knowledge you wish to achieve at the conclusion of your speech. Consider the following examples:

- The audience will know how to change a flat tire.
- The audience will know how to register to vote.
- At the conclusion of my speech the audience will sign a petition against rising gasoline taxes.
- The audience will believe that the appeal process for convicted murderers should be shortened.
- The audience will be amused with my story about canoeing.

Specific purpose statements follow the same guidelines whether they are for speeches to inform, persuade, or entertain. However, because of the intent of the speaker, they may be worded differently (primarily the verb you choose will be different). When you are giving a speech in which the general purpose is to inform, the specific purpose statement can begin with any of the following: "The audience will know . . . ." "The audience will understand . . ." "The audience will have a clear knowledge of . . . ." In a speech to persuade, the specific purpose statement should begin with, for example, "The audience will sign . . ." "The audience will donate . . ." and so forth.

It is important to note that you probably will not state your specific purpose statement during your speech. It is a tool to help you in creating your speech.

The importance of preparing a properly worded specific purpose statement should not be ignored. A well-worded, carefully prepared statement often makes the difference between a speech that is understood and a wandering monologue that reaches no one.

Strengthen Your Skills

Writing Specific Purpose Statements

Purpose: The purpose of this exercise is to give you practice in preparing different types of specific purpose statements.

Procedure:
Below you will find examples of specific purpose statements for focused speeches. You will create another specific purpose for that speech. Make sure it reflects the type of speech stated through the use of language:

Example:

Type of Speech: three- to five-minute informative speech

General Topic: Halloween

  a. The audience will know how to carve a jack-o-lantern.
  b. The audience will be able to make popcorn balls as treats for Halloween visitors.

Exercises:

1. Type of Speech: three- to five-minute informative speech
   General Topic: Snow
   a. The audience will know how to make a snowball.
   b. (you fill this in)

2. Type of Speech: three- to five-minute informative speech
   General Topic: Clothes
   a. The audience will be able to construct a wraparound skirt.
   b. (you fill this in)

3. Type of Speech: three- to five-minute informative speech
   General Topic: Zoos
   a. The audience will be aware of how the St. Louis Zoo is funded.
   b. (you fill this in)

(continued)

4. Type of Speech: five- to seven-minute persuasive speech

   General Topic: Valentine's Day

   a. The audience will send Valentine's Day cards to their loved ones.

   b. (you fill this in)

5. Type of Speech: five- to seven-minute persuasive speech

   General Topic: Cars

   a. The audience will purchase an economy car rather than an SUV.

   b. (you fill this in)

6. Type of Speech: five- to seven-minute persuasive speech

   General Topic: Cleaning

   a. The audience will use environmentally friendly cleaners.

   b. (you fill this in)

7. Type of Speech: three- to five-minute special occasion speech

   General Topic: Introduction

   a. The audience will be introduced to the school mascot.

   b. (you fill this in)

8. Type of Speech: three- to five-minute special occasion speech

   General Topic: Eulogy

   a. The audience will appreciate why my father was a special person.

   b. (you fill this in)

9. Type of Speech: three- to five-minute special occasion speech

   General Topic: Vacations

   a. The audience will be amused by the mishaps that occurred on my trip to Washington, DC.

   b. (you fill this in)

You have now learned how to create a specific purpose statement. This statement is a tool to help you and will be included as an item on your speech outline. In other words, this statement helps you know precisely what your speech goal is; now it's time to plan how you will reach it.

Conclusion

Remember that the sooner you pick a topic for your speech, the less anxiety you will feel. Make sure to focus your topic so that it "fits" all the criteria. This is an important step that you shouldn't skip. While creating a properly worded specific purpose statement may seem unimportant to the novice speaker it is actually an essential part of an effective speech. When you focus on the desired result you want from your audience, it helps you achieve your goal. Giving an effective speech requires much more than just telling the audience something. It demands that the speaker form a bond with the audience—that's what specific purpose statements can help you do.

Application to Everyday Life

You are probably thinking that there is no way you can use a specific purpose in your daily lives. That's not true; in fact, using what you have learned about a specific purpose can actually improve your daily communication quite a bit. When we know what our goals are, we are much more likely to achieve them. There are numerous conversations that take place daily that could benefit from considering their specific purpose. For example: Your anniversary is in two weeks and your spouse tends to forget to plan something (or sometimes even remember). If your specific purpose is, "My spouse will take me out to eat on our anniversary," you might end up at McDonald's! Being more specific, "My spouse will take me out to eat at Anthony's by the Pier on our anniversary," would more likely lead you into a clearer way to approach a conversation.

DISCUSSION QUESTIONS

1. List several methods of generating source ideas for speech topics.
2. Why should you avoid evaluation of topics during brainstorming? How does "hitchhiking" help?
3. What is focusing, and why is it essential to creating an effective speech?
4. Use an example to explain how data from your audience analysis is used to focus your speech for a specific audience.
5. Why isn't "I will tell my audience about my trip to the Alamo" a properly worded specific purpose statement? Why does the wording make a difference?

KEY WORDS

- brainstorming
- focusing
- general conversation
- hitchhiking
- specific purpose statement
- speech topic

7

Organizing Your Thoughts

- The introduction of your speech must be planned to be productive.
- A speaker must gain an audience's attention in the first few seconds of a speech.
- An effective introduction must fulfill four criteria.
- There are many creative ways to start a speech.
- The key to developing an organized speech body is through an outline.
- Your speech should be organized in a way that is orderly and easy for your audience to follow.
- There are several types of outlines; working outlines, speaking outlines, and formal outlines.
- The conclusion should be a clear statement that will help the audience remember the main points of your speech.
- Your conclusion should be about the same length as your introduction.
- An effective conclusion fulfills three criteria.
- There are many creative ways to end a speech.

Vice President Al Jones is working on his keynote address. Pam and John have provided him with some excellent information about all divisions of the company, their functions, and the employees who work at each division. He is surprised that he did not know much of the information and is impressed at how thorough the analysis is. He will need to make sure his speech is relevant to the whole company and that they find the information useful. He thinks he should tell them how the company was founded, past and present accomplishments of the company, and what the future holds. He will need to be very organized because Pam and John have given him only fifteen minutes to speak. He must buckle down and get to work.

CATEGORY: BORING SPEECHES
"My speech is about how to make a cherry pie."
"Today I'm going to tell you how to save money by using coupons."
"The topic of my speech is why you should wear your seat belts."
"Well that's about it."
"Are there any questions?"
"That's all."
"I'm done."
"Thank you."
Contestant: "What are truly bad ways to begin and end speeches?"
Alex: "That's correct for $1000."

Most people spend a great deal of time working on the body of their speech. They are concerned with getting their main points across. Yet they spend little time on the beginning (introduction) and ending (conclusion) of the speech. When that happens, speeches end up with boring introductions and conclusions like those mentioned in the *Jeopardy* example above.

Research shows that a speaker must gain the audience's attention in the first few seconds of a speech. It also shows that an audience listens best to the beginning and the end of a speech. Even though the body of your speech will use most of your speaking time, the introduction and conclusion are extremely important and must be carefully developed.

The Introduction

The *introduction* of your speech must be planned to ensure that you start your speech in a positive, productive manner. It should fill approximately 15 to 20 percent of your overall time limit. In this short time an introduction needs to be clever, creative, clear, and concise. An effective introduction must fulfill the following four criteria:

1. It should grab the audience's *attention*.
2. It will *inform* the audience of your topic.
3. It gives the audience a *reason to listen* by answering the question, "What's in it for me?" (WIFM).
4. It establishes the *credibility* of the speaker.

Getting the audience's attention is vitally important to accomplishing your speaking goal. If you don't grab their attention and get them to listen to you at the beginning of your speech, chances are you won't be able to catch them during your speech.

Bill began his speech by dropping a lit match into a wastebasket filled with paper. The materials took flame and set the sprinkler system off in the classroom. Obviously, evacuating was necessary. Though he grabbed the attention of his audience, they never knew that his topic was going to be stage lighting! Although he had their attention, he didn't fulfill all four criteria for an effective introduction!

The speaker must grab the audience's attention in the first few seconds of the speech.

Your introduction should get your audience to pay attention to you, but it must also inform the audience of your topic. This brings us back to the "bad" examples with which we started this section. Obviously those fairly typical "My topic is . . ." introductions fulfill the purpose of letting your audience know what the general topic is, but they don't grab the audience members' attention. In fact, they will probably have the opposite effect and cause the audience to tune out. Remember the entertainment syndrome? Do not fall into the trap of only listening to things you find interesting. As a speaker you must be aware that many of your audience members will be operating in this mode. It's your job as a speaker to get them listening. Find an interesting way to introduce them to your topic, use a *grabber* to gain their attention.

The third requirement for an effective introduction is *WIFM* (What's in it for me). The me, refers to the audience. You must assume that your audience is questioning whether they will gain anything by listening to your speech. By answering this question you can ensure that your audience will listen to you. WIFM lets you tell the audience that there will be a reward if they pay attention. For example, listeners might learn an inexpensive way to entertain their children or a new idea for that perfect date. You can't just make up a reward and expect it to be effective. The reward must be one the audience will want, so this is another instance in the speech process where an audience analysis pays off. Audience analysis allows you to discover the needs, wants, and desires the audience has that your speech can help fulfill. Using this information early in your speech catches your audience's attention up front and ensures they continue to listen.

As you plan your introduction, you can usually create an attention grabber that also serves the purpose of informing your audience about your topic. The WIFM statement is actually fairly easy to incorporate if you have done a thorough audience analysis and you know your topic well enough. With those three steps completed you are ready to finalize your introduction. You must make sure the audience perceives you as credible. Establishing your *credibility* is one aspect of an introduction that may seem like a stumbling block.

A speaker's credibility can be established based on his or her knowledge of the subject. However, the audience's perception of the speaker's trustworthiness, and how they judge the speaker's personal appearance, also influence whether or not the audience believes the speaker to be credible. Speakers who take the time to establish their credibility up front are much more effective.

Your credibility will continue to be built throughout your speech. However, you can help to establish a foundation for it by explaining your competence about your subject in your introduction. What's your experience with this topic? Where did you get your information? Be honest and careful when presenting your information—don't distort, lie, or leave out vital information. Is this a hobby you have been doing since you were a child? Tell the audience. Is this a disease that you or a family member suffers from? Tell the audience. Is this something you have had an interest in for years and have done extensive research about? Tell the audience. This will provide your audience with accurate, reliable information and establish your credibility in the first few seconds of your speech. Your goal is to show them why listening to you is important. You want your audience to be concerned, excited, happy, or angry about your topic. This motivates them to continue to listen.

Creating an effective introduction may seem impossible in such a relatively short time, but it isn't. It is often your attention grabber that is the most difficult item to develop. The following is a list of possible grabbers you could use to begin your speech but be as creative as you like—just make sure to place your grabber first, and that your entire introduction fulfills the four requirements you have just learned.

1. Give an example or tell a story.

    a. "My mother was ironing; I was playing with my doll." "I was four years old the day John F. Kennedy was assassinated."

    b. "Teaching someone how to do something is often the best way to help yourself learn. For example, I've been studying algebra and think I don't understand it. My younger brother is taking a beginning course and is struggling with his homework assignment. I helped him by explaining the basic theories. I discovered that I really do understand algebra, after all. Teaching my brother helped me learn!"

2. Ask your audience a question.

    a. "Have you ever wondered if your great-grandchildren will vacation on the moon?"

    b. Is New Orleans the most haunted city in America?

3. Present a quotation.

    a. "'Don't try it! I've tried them all myself and they don't work.' This is what my uncle always said when he first spoke to new 'boots' at Great Lakes Naval Training Base."

b. "As Mark Twain said, 'I have never let my schooling interfere with my education.'"

4. Refer to a historical event or date.

   a. "September 11, 2001, is no longer just a fall day. It is a day we, as Americans, will never forget."

   b. "It was on this day in 1775 that the American Revolution began. A single shot fired at Concord Bridge became a shot heard round the world."

5. Tell a joke. (Make sure it is related to your topic.)

   a. For a speech on shearing sheep, you might start with, "Where do sheep get their hair cut? At baaaber shops."

   b. If you are giving a speech on the importance of enunciating your words and speaking clearly, you might start with, "As a newly released prisoner was running through the prison gates he yelled, 'I'm free, I'm free!' A child playing nearby responded, 'Big deal! I'm four!'"

6. State an unusual fact.

   a. "Your neighbor, your friend, a member of your family—one out of every two people in America is emotionally disturbed or mentally ill."

   b. "By the year 2020, one out of four adults will have, or know someone with, AIDS."

7. Use a gimmick (a novelty opening).

   a. Do a sleight-of-hand trick that changes a dollar bill into thirty-five cents to begin a speech on inflation.

   b. Dress as Count Dracula for a speech on blood donation or vampires.

8. Refer to the purpose of your gathering. This works best when the audience is already emotionally aroused about the topic, such as a board meeting or company policy review.

   a. "Five children have been injured while crossing the street in front of this grade school. We must have patrolled crosswalks. Our children's futures, maybe their lives, depend on it!"

   b. "February is the month for love. Valentine's Day is the most profitable day in the floral business. We can sell even more flowers selling love."

Strengthen Your Skills

The Introduction

Purpose: The purpose of this exercise is to learn how to prepare a speech introduction that uses all four criteria we have learned.

Procedure:

1. Bring a short news article or magazine article to class (or the instructor may hand out articles).

2. Select one of the eight grabbers and prepare an introduction for your article. Make sure it fulfills all four requirements for an effective introduction.

   a. It gains the audience's attention (grabber).

   b. It informs the audience of your topic.

   c. It gives the audience a reason to listen, by answering their question, "What's in it for me?"

   d. It establishes your credibility.

3. The introduction should be forty seconds to one minute in length and cannot start with, "My speech is about . . ."

4. Present the introduction orally in class or write it out and submit it to your instructor.

Organizing the Speech Body

We've often heard students say, "I can prepare a speech, but I can't do the outline until last." Quite honestly, this is backwards! The key to developing a well-prepared speech is organization, and organizing your speech means arranging it in a way that is easy for your audience to follow. *Outlining* is the process used to achieve this goal. Those who skip this process usually present a speech that rambles and is difficult to follow. Learning to prepare an outline can provide these advantages.

- The information in your speech becomes more familiar as you organize it, helping you to remember your speech material.

- You will be more relaxed, knowing you are organized and prepared.

- Your audience will be able to follow what you say because your speech moves logically from point to point.

- A proper organizational pattern creates a natural adjustment mechanism that lets your audience process information.

- Your audience will remember what you say because organized information makes sense.

There are several types of outlines. *Working outlines* are used when you are working on your speech. They help you organize your ideas by putting your information in writing. They can help you determine what to include as support for the points of your speech. A working outline may be a series of phrases you have jotted down during the preparation process as you analyze your audience or do your research. These outlines can be created in any way you choose that is easy for you to follow. Your working outline will probably be seen only by you and does not need to follow any specific style.

A *speaking outline* is the outline you will take to the podium. Speaking outlines are also personal. Again, you can use any format that works best for you. Using an outline at the podium can help jog your memory and keep you from rambling while speaking. In addition, you can write notes to yourself about delivery or write transition words between points. If you use your speaking outline as your speaking notes, it's often a good idea to transfer it to note cards.

A *formal outline* is the one you will most likely be required to present to your instructor when you actually deliver your speech. This must conform to certain rules. The main points of your speech are noted by Roman numerals (I, II, III). The subpoints of your speech are noted by capital letters (A, B, C). Further subpoints are noted by Arabic numbers (1, 2, 3), and any further division by lowercase letters (a, b, c). If you find it necessary to divide a point further, it probably means that your point is too broad and needs to be more clearly focused.

The most common mistake made by beginning speakers is trying to include too much information in the body of their speech. Research suggests that the body of your speech should contain no more than three to five main points. These main points will be represented by Roman numerals in your outline. Concentrate on the most important points and develop each of them fully. This will result in a thorough and organized outline.

Preparing a Formal Outline

We suggest that all outlines should list your speech's specific purpose statement first. Then, when preparing a formal outline, you must label the three major parts of your presentation, the introduction, the body, and the conclusion. This assures that you have considered the purpose of each section of the speech. In addition, you should list your *bibliography* (sources) on your outline. A formal speech outline looks like this:

Specific Purpose Statement

Introduction

    I. Grabber statement (gains audience's attention).

   II. Statement that informs the audience of your topic.

III. WIFM (gives the audience a reason to listen by answering the question: what's in it for me?)

IV. Statement that establishes your credibility.

Body

    I. Main point #1

    Subpoints

    II. Main point #2

    Subpoints

    III. Main point #3 (continue until all points are listed, with no more than 5)

    Subpoints

Conclusion

    I. Review the main ideas.

    II. Statement that refers back to your grabber and lets the audience know you are finished.

Bibliography

    I. Source #1

    II. Source #2

    III. Source #3

    (continue listing all sources)

When selecting the main points of your speech, you must take into account the primary (most important) sections of your speech. They should be equal in importance and fill about the same amount of time in your presentation. *Example:* You are giving a speech about purebred cats. The main points in the body of your speech might look like this:

    I. Siamese

    II. Persian

    III. Himalayan

Subpoints (capital letters—A, B, etc.) would then be added and would represent a division of your main points; as they further explain those points. These should also be of equal importance to each other and relate specifically to the heading under which they fall. In the same way, further subpoints (Arabic numerals—1, 2, etc.) fill the requirement of dividing the category under which they fall. The process of outlining involves breaking down broad ideas into smaller ones. Each time you divide an idea you must break it down into at least two parts. Simply stated, this means that every time you have a I, you must have at least a II; if you have an A, you must have a B; for every 1 there must be a 2.

Occasionally, you may find that some of your supporting material does not easily fall into two or more sections. When this occurs you simply identify the material under its heading. This is done by labeling such as example, story, quotation, definition, or visual aid—followed by a colon, and the material itself.

Here is an example:

A. Helping others

Quotation: President Barack Obama on volunteering in one's community.

Each division or point on your outline should list only one idea. Don't put two or more ideas together. It is a good idea to list your topic, general purpose, time frame (how long you will be allowed for delivery), and your specific purpose statement on your outline. Let's look at an example of how the previously discussed guidelines for a formal speech outline might look.

Topic: How to Change a Flat Tire

General Purpose: Informative Speech

Time Frame: 5–7 minutes

Specific Purpose: The audience will know how to change a flat tire.

Introduction

    I. Tell a story about changing tire in freezing weather without a jack.

    II. Changing a flat tire can be an easy procedure with the right equipment.

    III. (WIFM) It can save you time and money in the future.

    IV. I have had to change a flat tire six times.

Body

    I. Equipment

       A. Tire Tool

       Visual Aid: show tool

       B. Jack

          1. Type A (bumper)

          2. Type B (scissors)

       C. Spare Tire

    II. Procedure

       A. Securing the Vehicle

          1. Pull car off road.

    2. Make car immovable.

       a. Put transmission in park.

       b. Block wheels.

       Example: blocks or bricks

  B. Removing the Flat Tire

    1. Remove hubcap.

    2. Loosen lug nuts.

    3. Jack up car.

    4. Remove tire.

  C. Replacing the Tire

    1. Put wheel on rim.

    2. Replace lug nuts.

    3. Release jack.

    4. Tighten lug nuts.

    5. Replace hubcap.

  D. Finishing the Job

    1. Put equipment away.

    2. Remove wheel blocks.

III. Follow-up

  A. Go to the nearest service station.

    1. Have lug nuts tightened.

    2. Check air pressure in spare.

    3. Have flat fixed.

  B. Replace spare with fixed tire.

<u>Conclusion</u>

  I. Now you know the equipment and procedure for changing a tire.

  II. Follow these steps and you won't be left in freezing weather with a flat tire like I was!

<u>Bibliography</u>

  Source 1

  Source 2, etc.

Notice the form of the outline, where to indent, when to capitalize, and where to put periods. Outlines can be written using words and phrases or full sentences. Most people find the word/phrase outline easier, but many beginning speakers like the added security of a full-sentence outline. Whichever style you choose, be consistent. Use phrases *or* sentences throughout the outline; don't use the two interchangeably.

An outline of a speech is much like a map. You want it to be clear. Your outline maps and directs the flow of your speech and includes all the information you will use to achieve your specific purpose. There are many organizational patterns that can help you outline and order your speech.

Organizational Patterns

There are many ways of mapping and ordering your main points. The most important thing to remember is to prepare your outline so that your speech will move from point to point in a logical manner, one that is easy for your audience to follow. Here are possible *organizational patterns* you can use for your speech.

Chronological organization organizes your material in a specific time frame. What occurred first, second, third? You move from the first occurrence to the most recent occurrence. If you were speaking on the development of our money system, chronological divisions might look like this:

    I.   Ancient Barter System

    II. Early Roman Coinage

    III. English Money

    IV. Colonial Money

    V.   Modern Money

All the divisions are organized in time order, whether by years, months, or minutes.

Spatial organization uses divisions that are made according to geographical areas or space. If you were speaking about taking a trip from New York to California, spatial divisions might be:

    I.   Leave eastern seaboard

    II. Drive to Midwest

    III. Continue to mountains

    IV. Arrive on West Coast

Remember, spatial divisions involve progressing from place to place or geographical location.

Process organization is used when you wish to follow a series of step-by-step actions. An outline showing the process for how to bake a cake could be handled in this way:

    I.   Read the recipe.

    II. Collect the ingredients and utensils.

    III. Mix the ingredients.

    IV. Bake the cake.

    V.   Serving suggestions.

Any topic that requires step-by-step action can be organized using a process division.

Priority organization separates items by importance, least to most important or vice-versa. You must decide how to prioritize your points. An outline on personal hygiene, organized by what you believe to be the most important element followed by the least important, could look like this:

    I. Bathing

   II. Deodorant

  III. Cosmetics

Causal organization shows a relationship between the cause and effect of a topic. This type of pattern is often used for persuasive speeches to show what needs to be changed to bring about a particular result. An outline for a speech on the effects of viewing TV violence might look like this.

    I. Children's television programs have been found to contain a high percentage of violence.

   II. Studies show that viewing violence affects children's behavior.

  III. Violent crimes are increasing among children.

Problem solution organization discusses certain changes that need to occur and then offers a solution to achieve these changes.

    I. Animals are killed to provide fur for coats.

   II. Methods of killing these animals are cruel.

  III. Human beings don't need fur for coats.

  IV. Banning the sale of fur coats would end the unnecessary death of animals.

Strengthen Your Skills

Ordering Points

Purpose: The purpose of this exercise is to give you an opportunity to gain experience in organizing data.

Procedure:
Organize the following statements in a logical order:

- A goal can be a dream.
- Society has failed many because they can't achieve their goals.
- Everyone needs a dream.
- Without dreams we become apathetic.
- Without the ability to achieve our goals, we lose hope.
- Society needs dreamers.

These are just a few of the ways you can divide and organize your topic. You might want to consider the pros and cons of each, choosing the one most relevant to your topic. Just make sure that the pattern you choose helps the flow of your speech. The speech must move logically and smoothly from point to point.

The last thing you must include in your outline is your list of sources. This should be done in standard bibliography format, which will be covered later in the text. The number of sources you need for a particular speech will vary.

With a well-organized outline, the body of your speech is ready to become part of your presentation. Here is a summary of what to do to write an outline:

1. Decide on your main points.

2. Divide the main points, where necessary, into further subcategories.

3. Decide on an organizational pattern.

4. Add your introduction, conclusion, and sources.

Strengthen Your Skills

Outlining

Purpose: The purpose of this exercise is for you to learn how to write a formal outline.

Procedure:

1. Outline a manuscript speech recommended by your instructor. You may use a full sentence outline or a word/phrase outline.

2. Submit your outline to your instructor for comments and corrections.

Conclusions

Now that you have thought about how to begin your speech and what you will say during it, you must create a *conclusion.* Since this is the last thing your audience will hear, you want to leave them with a clear statement so they will remember the main points of your speech. A conclusion should take about the same amount of time as your introduction. An effective conclusion must fulfill three criteria:

1. It should clearly remind the audience of your topic and main points.

2. It notifies the audience that you have finished your speech.

3. It should be linked to your introduction.

Just as your introduction informs your audience members what you are going to tell them, your conclusion tells them that you have said it. You should make a clear statement that reviews the main points of your speech. Conclude your speech in a way that will make clear to the members of your audience what you wanted them to learn. You want them to remember specific points. Don't leave them guessing.

Let your audience know that you are finished speaking. Don't say, "That's about it, are there any questions?" Don't add any new information in your conclusion. Once you've started your conclusion and signaled a stop, don't ramble; tie it up (even if you left out some point when you were speaking). Make sure you show that the information you have been relating all works together to arrive at this particular ending. Your final statement should be tied to your introduction and, in fact, can be prepared in the same way as your grabber. You can conclude with any of the following, so choose a creative ending.

1. A question
2. A quotation
3. A historical event
4. An example
5. A joke
6. An unusual fact
7. A gimmick

Strengthen Your Skills

The Conclusion

Purpose: The purpose of this exercise is to learn how to prepare a speech conclusion.

Procedure:

1. Bring a short news article to class (or the instructor may hand out articles to read).

2. Referring to the different ways to end a speech in this chapter, prepare a conclusion for the article. Make sure it fulfills the three criteria.

   a. It reminds the audience of your topic and main points.

   b. It notifies the audience that you have finished.

   c. It should tie back to your introduction.

3. The conclusion should be forty seconds to one minute in length.

4. Present the conclusion in class or write it down and submit it to your instructor for comments.

The thing you don't want your listeners to remember about your speech is that they were confused when you stopped speaking and didn't know you were finished.

Conclusion

Introductions and conclusions, while only a small part of your speech are essential elements in reaching your audience. While they are often ignored by novice speakers, effective speakers know their importance and spend time in developing them. Organization is also key to the delivery of an effective speech that gets and keeps your audience's attention. A detailed, complete outline will help you achieve your specific goal.

Application to Everyday Life

You're probably wondering if you will ever use your knowledge of how to outline ever again. We'd like to show you how the skills learned in this chapter could improve your day-to-day life. The purpose of outlining is organization. In learning to identify main points and support them, we've learned how things can be organized in a logical fashion. Outlining your speeches provides us an opportunity to think about what the main points are, what can be moved to a supportive position, and even what should be eliminated. When these skills are applied to organizing our day-to-day priorities, we can expect the same outcome.

You have all probably prepared a to-do list (or had someone make one for you). Usually this list is composed of several chores and/or errands that need to be accomplished within a certain time period. However, if you look closely, you'll find that those items actually fall into different categories of priority. Some tasks need to be done within twenty-four hours; others don't need to be completed immediately, some need to be finished within the week; still others may not get completed at all (like cleaning the attic or basement). Making a priority list in outline fashion can ease stress, help you with time management, and keep you from feeling guilty about those items you never seem to have time to complete!

Take a few moments to write or think about your to-do list. What categories could you divide those tasks into?

DISCUSSION QUESTIONS

1. What are the four criteria an introduction should fulfill? Why are they necessary for an effective introduction?

2. Using a topic of your choice, prepare five different ways of gaining the audience's attention for introducing the same topic and explain the effectiveness of each.

3. Prepare three different ways of concluding the same speech topic.

4. What benefits can be derived from the creation of a working outline for your speech?

5. What is the difference between a working outline and a formal outline?

KEY WORDS

- bibliography
- causal organization
- chronological organization
- conclusion
- credibility
- formal outline
- grabber
- introduction
- organizational patterns
- outlining
- priority organization
- problem solution organization
- process organization
- spatial organization
- speaking outline
- working outline
- WIFM

8

Just the Facts, Please

Research

- Time spent learning facts, clarifying ideas, and finding examples during the research process will save time later.
- Research supports your ideas, giving your audience a reason to believe what you say.
- Taking time to prepare a research plan now will save you time later.
- In a research plan you consider what information you need, why you need it, and where you are likely to find it.
- There are many types of support you can use for your speech.
- Avoid plagiarism by citing your sources in your speech.
- There are many possible sources to use to find support for your topic both on- and off-line.
- There are five things you should consider when deciding what references to use in your speech.
- You know your references are reliable and credible by doing a credibility check, which is as simple as A (authority), B (bias), C (content/currency), D (design).
- A wiki is software that allows for quick and easy collaboration in a document. Its greatest asset (multiple people can edit a document) is also its greatest liability. How do you know if it is reliable?

Barry Foster has spent the last several days on the computer. He has been collecting facts about various computer software vendors and their manufacturing programs. He has been assigned the task of informing the employees of the entire company about the new computer software program that they will be using next year. Although he has used the software before, he wants to be sure the information he shares with them is current and accurate. There are a few things that he is still unsure about. Maybe he will call the company's customer service hotline and ask them some additional questions. Better safe than sorry!

Why do I need to research my topic? Why can't I just talk about what I know? Why should I use research when I already know what I want to say? The answers to these questions depend entirely on the circumstances surrounding your speech. There are times when you will have no time for research. Does this mean you don't share your ideas? Of course not. You collect your thoughts, quickly organize them, and then you deliver your speech. On the other hand, most speaking engagements will be known in advance, allowing you time to research your topic.

Why Research?

There are entire courses devoted to how to do research. Many of you have already taken a course that required you to write a research paper. If you have completed such a course, this chapter will serve as a review. If you haven't, this unit will give you some basic information on why research is necessary and can show you how to find support for your speeches. In addition, we urge you to check out the many excellent Web sites that offer information and tutorials on researching.

Time spent learning facts, clarifying ideas, and finding examples during the research process will save you time later. Though you may believe you're well informed about your topic, you will most likely find that you still need additional information. You may need to do an experiment, gather data, read about a peace treaty, verify the wording of a law, or check an ingredient in Mom's sweet pickle recipe. You may need a chart, story, or recording to help clarify, explain, or add interest to your speech. Whatever your speech is about, adding information to what you already know will help you decide what else you need to include. You may discover that some material is not as important as you thought, or discover you neglected to include some major or interesting point. Frequently, researching your topic leads you to rewrite your specific purpose statement, making your presentation clearer.

One of the most important reasons for doing research is to make sure you are relaying correct and current information. However, you won't know for sure until you have researched and verified this information. Perpetuating misinformation can confuse your audience. Researching your data helps you to avoid this problem.

Research supports your ideas, giving your audience a reason to believe what you say. Citing your sources during your speech is one of the primary ways speakers create credibility with an audience. Researching involves collecting examples, quotes, statistics, and any other material you need to share with your audience so that they will believe you. As you gather and prepare your material, look for items that will prove and illustrate your points.

The Research Plan

"Proper Planning Prevents Poor Performance" is an adage more of us should learn and apply. We're busy people. We don't even want to pull over and wait for our fast-food order. How many of you have stopped the microwave at the last ten seconds because that was just too long to wait? So, we certainly don't have the time or inclination to spend "planning" research. It wastes time. We can just boot up the computer or head for the nearest library. If we start researching immediately, we can move on with our project, paper, or speech. There's no time to waste—just do it! Right?

Take a look at the first sentence of this section again. It's time to confess. How many times have you rushed into something without thinking it through and regretted it? How many times have you had to make an additional trip to complete a chore you forgot about when you were out earlier in the day? How many times have you had to do something over because you didn't follow directions the first time? How much time have you wasted because you failed to plan before doing something? Your authors think that collectively we have probably wasted several years of our lives. Taking time to prepare a research plan now will save you time later! In a *research plan*, you consider what information you need, why you need it, and where you are likely to find it. An effective research plan will address three general areas:

1. Topic
2. Audience analysis
3. Data needed

While your authors suggest you take time (probably only a few minutes) to write out your research plan, this step can be done mentally. The format you use is your choice since no one will see it except you (unless your instructor wants a copy). For each area of your plan, you will need to ask yourself several questions. The answers to these questions will direct your research.

The Topic

By this time in the process you should have created a specific purpose statement that considers you, the audience, and the occasion. If you haven't done so, you aren't ready to research. Once you have your specific purpose, ask yourself the following questions:

1. What is the overall topic of my speech?
2. What is the specific topic of my speech?
3. What are other related topics?
4. What else could these topics be called?

The purpose of considering these questions is to give you an idea as to what kind of sources you might need. It's also important if you are going to be using the Internet. Knowing your general topic will help you decide whether you are going online, heading to a museum, or planning an interview. Knowing your specific topic will help you fine-tune exactly what you actually need to look up once your general topic is located. Knowing other related topics can help expand a search that isn't providing what you need. Knowing other names for a topic will help you find additional information more easily. We've known students who insist (and we believe them) that they have spent hours trying to find two or three sources to support a five- to seven-minute speech, yet can't find anything about their topic. They often think they have to change their topic and start all over again! They're frustrated and angry that they've wasted so much time. As their teachers, we ask if they took the time to prepare a research plan. The answer is usually no, because if they had, they would have gone to question 4 and considered what else their topic could be called. We have frequently found that when we type in a different word for their topic in our favorite search engine, we are rewarded with a multitude of Web sites that offer valuable information.

Audience Analysis

Previously we emphasized the importance of an audience analysis. If you did one for your topic, then answering the questions related to this step should be easy. If you can't answer these questions, go back and look at your audience analysis again. If you don't have enough information to answer these questions, you must seek additional information about your audience before you can continue with your research. You should be able to answer these questions to guide your research plan:

- What knowledge does my audience have about my topic?
- What needs does my audience have that I can fulfill by the time I reach my conclusion?
- How can I keep my audience interested in my topic?

Since these are similar questions to those that you asked in your audience analysis, you should find you have enough information already for this part of the research plan. Knowing how much your audience already knows about your topic will help you focus your search for specific materials. If your topic is one that they already know something about, you must find new information that is unfamiliar to your audience.

Knowing what your audience's needs are is an essential ingredient for any effective speech. Not only is this the way you get their attention initially (WIFM), but it is how you maintain it throughout your speech. Where can you find the information that will fulfill their needs? What kind of support is required to convince your audience that your speech will provide them with a reward? This is where you might use that list of related topics you generated in the first step of this process. If your topic is saving money, what additional sources might help you get your audience to realize the need to save?

Finally, consider finding any additional information that can keep your audience interested in your topic. Would a clever quote, poem, or example help? Where are you likely to find sources for these elements? Would a pie chart help explain those numbers you need to include? Do you need an audio clip to help your audience understand what you are explaining? Would a list of Web sites be an appropriate handout, or do you need clear directions on how to make recipe? Did Oprah or Dr. Phil do a TV program on your topic? Did you record it? Can it be found at Oprah.com? Considering what you need to enhance your speech makes it much more likely that you can keep your audience interested.

If you are planning a *persuasive speech*, you might additionally need to counteract any ideas or opinions the audience already has about your topic. Do they have emotional attachments that you need to consider in order to persuade them? How can you establish credibility?

A research plan can help you discover the specific information you will need to establish and support your topic or arguments. You won't waste time researching information that doesn't relate to your topic.

The Data Needed

After you have answered the questions about the topic and the audience analysis, you should have a clear idea of the *specific* information you need to enhance your topic. In fact, if you have done a really thorough analysis of the topic and the audience, you may not need to complete this section of your research plan at all. This part of the plan lists possible sources you need to check to support your speech and establish credibility.

Even if you have mentally thought through the previous two steps, it's a good idea to write down the answers to the following questions:

- What sources will provide the information I need?
- Where will I find them?
- How much time do I *need* to find this information?

Since you have most likely chosen a topic you are interested in and know something about, chances are you already know some specific sources to check. Write them down. Can this be a "one-stop" shopping trip? Can you get all the information you need at the local library, or will you need to plan online time *and* an interview with a friend? Plan it out. Make sure you provide yourself adequate time to complete the actual research once you know what it is you wish to find. This is similar to the way executives plan for a business meeting!

Since we started this chapter by discussing our busy lives, it seems obvious that your research plan should include a step that considers how much time will be needed to complete your research. Also consider how much time you will need to read, analyze, organize, and prepare the information you gather into an effective speech. Try to make a good estimate of how much time needs to be allotted for each aspect of the research. If you have three hours to get things done, your research plan will be different than if you have eight hours to spend on your speech preparation process. Be realistic and narrow your search if necessary to fit your time constraints.

If you have adequately focused your topic, it won't take you long to prepare a research plan. Thirty minutes or less will find you with a plan in hand that will save you an enormous amount of time. You might spend hours conducting useless research without a plan! Once you have your plan, you will find that there are many types of support you can use for your speech.

The following is a list of the types of support you might look for while researching your speech:

- Examples
- Illustrations
- Explanations
- Descriptions
- Analogies
- Statistics
- Opinions
- Testimony
- Numerical Data

- Facts
- Quotations
- Comparisons
- Contrasts
- Graphs
- Charts
- Tables
- Photographs

While statistics can be effective in supporting your ideas, there are some things you should be careful to check before presenting them to your audience. Make sure you aren't misrepresenting the numbers; you must provide them completely, and never use them out of context. Make sure the source is unbiased and the statistics are recent; verify them with other sources if possible. Any support that involves numbers needs to be handled carefully.

Numbers tend to be abstract concepts to many people. How many is a billion? Provide an example that helps make them more concrete, something that will help your audience visualize the concept you are presenting. To explain the "numbers served" they so proudly display on their signs, McDonald's might effectively use concrete examples in its advertising. They could say that if you laid all the hamburgers they've sold end to end, they would reach all the way to the moon and back again, or they would circle the equator a certain number of times. We can understand these examples better than the concept of "billions." Finally, don't overuse or misuse statistics. A speech that contains too many numbers is difficult for audiences to follow. Examples are usually more effective than too many statistics.

Citing Your Sources

It is important to give credit where credit is due. Researchers spend many hours validating and publishing their ideas. It is important to pay tribute to their commitment. Students often find themselves in trouble when they present information they have researched in oral or written form, due to plagiarism. *Plagiarism* is, simply stated, stealing someone else's work. This happens when students get into a bind and deliberately copy someone else's work and then present it as their own. However, most plagiarism occurs because a student is not sure how to present the information that he or she has gathered. The student either uses the author's exact words without mentioning the source, or paraphrases the main ideas without giving credit to the author. You can avoid this problem by citing all your sources and indicating when you use a quote. This is easy to do. You simply say during your speech, "According to (the organization or people who conducted the research) a study done in (give year), found that (your point). If you are in doubt about whether you are plagiarizing, ask your instructor. Never take credit for something that isn't your own work. Since you won't be writing out your speech, you'll need to state your sources orally during your speech as you mention the data you researched.

Although some speeches draw on your own knowledge, very often that knowledge originated with another source. After all, someone showed you how to change the oil in your car, you learned how to keyboard from a manual, or your "original" recipe started with a basic one. Giving credit to the original source of your information is necessary to build your credibility with your audience. There are many possible sources to use to find support for your topic.

Sources: Tapping the Realm of Information

We are going to assume that the majority of you use the *Internet* on a daily basis. We suspect that you use it to check your e-mail, your Facebook page, chat with friends, or see what's new on your favorite site. So you've already used it for research. Your authors, having completed our degrees when a web was something a spider made, have nonetheless whole heartedly embraced the opportunities the World Wide Web provides. We can stay at home and teach our classes in our pajamas, or communicate with our friends, coworkers, and students online. In fact, the revisions for this edition of the text were completed while Mary was in the Midwest and Tracey was in the Pacific Northwest. We made this possible by sharing files electronically. Obviously, we will encourage you to use this valuable source. However, before you boot up and start Googling, remember that finding good sources takes more than Google.

The Internet

Why travel to a library when the computer in my home office can provide everything I need? To this we say, indeed! In all honesty, one of your authors hasn't checked anything out of the library in years! But just because most information is available through the Internet, it doesn't mean all of that information is credible or reliable.

The Internet is not really tangible, it's not a place, it's an idea. It consists of a very large number of people, all over the globe. Connected to phone lines, cable, and satellites through their computers, they have generated a vast amount of data and information. The Internet is just waiting for you, 24 hours a day, 365 days a year. Yet, much of what is out there is personal opinion.

To use the Internet, you need hardware that links computers through a telephone line, cable, or satellite; an Internet server (a service that you pay to provide access) and a Web browser (software that lets your computer find information). If you don't own a computer (or know someone who will let you use his/hers), don't despair. You aren't locked out of using the Net. Most colleges and universities, and many libraries, have computers available for use. Once you are in front of the computer, you are only a few mouse clicks away from beginning your search.

Search engines and directories provide easy ways of finding information about your topic. These free services search the Web to find sites that match the topic you entered. You can choose and access the ones you want. It's easy and very user-friendly. Don't assume that the sites listed first are the best.

You may know an *Internet address* (URL; an acronym that stands for uniform resource locator and is used synonymously with Internet address), find one in a magazine, or see one on TV. Carefully copy the *entire* address *exactly* as it appears. Your Web browser can take you to the site only if you give it the right address. If the address is not exact, you'll get an error message saying the destination could not be found. Sometimes you may find that the site no longer exists or that it requires a password and therefore can't be accessed. Don't be discouraged because there are all kinds of additional sites "out there"; you'll find dictionaries, newspapers, encyclopedias, magazines (often called "zines" on the Internet), and much more. You can surf to the White House, tour the Smithsonian, or search libraries all over the world. While the Internet is a potential source for vast amounts of information, you shouldn't believe everything you see.

If you own a PC (personal computer) with a modem, you don't even have to leave home to find excellent sources for your speech. You can think of the Internet as a huge library without paper, where search engines and directories serve as the library catalog. It's a wonderful source for research, so click and explore. Just be choosy about what you find!

Personal Experience: Yours and Others

You may not qualify as the world's leading authority on welfare reform, or the mating habits of tigers, but you have probably accumulated a great deal of knowledge during your lifetime. *Personal experience* is the ideal starting point for gaining support for your speech. You've chosen a topic you are interested in, and that means you have some knowledge about it. Indeed, you may be the primary source for some speeches you will give. You could easily teach your audience how to make brownies from a recipe you've used hundreds of times. You could talk about dealing with stress while going to school, working, and taking care of a family. You could explain how to change the oil in a car or how to install new software on a computer. If you've dealt with a topic and have experience with it, your personal knowledge is certainly one valid source for your speech. Although it's a good starting point, your experience probably isn't complete enough to serve as your only source.

In one class a student presented a persuasive speech on safe sex. This is a topic that most of the audience had heard about in detail and they thought much of the information wasn't going to be new. However, throughout her speech the student related new facts and statistics about the dangers of unprotected sexual encounters. In her conclusion as she implored the audience members to practice safe sex, she made her final statement one of personal experience. She said, "You see, I'm one of those statistics. I'm seventeen, unmarried, and the mother of a three-month-old baby girl." Using current facts and personalizing her speech had a dramatic effect, and this point is what convinced her audience to adhere to her advice.

People you know and interact with every day can also be wonderful sources for your speech. Suppose you are talking about the Vietnam War. You may be too young to have experienced that time in our nation's history. How can you understand yet alone convey the mood of our country during this time? You might know someone who was there, and his or her recollections could add valuable information to your speech. In fact, human experiences are much more interesting than statistics or dry historical facts. Take advantage of the wealth of information available to you from people you see and talk to every day.

Interviews

Conducting an *interview* is a research method by which you question people who are knowledgeable in a field of study. This allows you to take advantage of expert opinions and knowledge. Interviews can be conducted in person, on the telephone, or by e-mail. These are an excellent source to use for information that might not be available from other sources.

Don't just stop by someone's office. Call him or her on the phone and request an interview. Make an appointment. Explain who you are and why you want the interview. This initial contact also provides an opportunity for you to ask if you can record the interview. Do your homework, find out about your expert interviewee, and decide what information you need from him or her. Don't arrive at the interview and say, "Tell me what you know about gardening." Rather, ask questions that relate directly to your speech. It is a good idea to write down any questions that you want to ask before you go to the interview. Sending them in advance to your interviewee is the best method and allows him or her time to prepare for your visit. That way, you will not waste time and will be well organized. Make notes on what is said even if you are recording the conversation (machines sometimes fail to work). Pay attention to your time and try not to take up more time than was scheduled. Be sure to thank the person for the interview and give him or her credit as one of your sources in your speech and on your outline.

Strengthen Your Skills

Interviewing

Purpose: This exercise will give you experience interviewing.

Procedure: Choose a topic and conduct a personal interview as support material. Pick a person who is knowledgeable in this area to interview.

1. Make an appointment to see this person. During this initial call, ask if you may record or videotape the interview.

2. Develop questions (probably 4 or 5) that you can ask and expand on during the interview. If possible, send your questions in advance to allow the interviewee time to prepare.

3. Interview your subject.

4. Write a simple thank you note to this person (e-mail is acceptable) after your interview session.

5. Use the information as a source of support for your speech if applicable.

Surveys

Surveys are designed to gather information from a large number of people. A survey asks specific questions relating to a specific topic. Surveys may request factual data or ask for opinions. There are four ways to gather information in a survey: you can mail a questionnaire, conduct a survey by phone, conduct a survey in person, or ask questions via the Internet. The Internet offers several forums in which you can contact respondents, such as chat rooms and instant messaging. Also, some Web sites may provide bulletin boards or asynchronous discussion areas where you can post questions and people can reply with their answers. In fact, you can often find surveys that have already been conducted and use their results as support for your topic.

Developing a survey requires some work and attention to detail. Survey questions can be written in many different ways, depending on your purpose for asking the question. You may want to ask questions that require only a "yes" or "no" answer or you may want to give the respondent a choice of multiple answers! In addition to questions that address your specific topic, you should ask questions pertaining to a respondents' demographic background (i.e., age, occupation, gender, etc.). Demographic information provides a helpful means of categorizing the answers you receive.

You will also have to select a sample group (people whom you will question) that are representative of the population you want to know about. Looking for opinions on voting? You can probably find a representative sample of voters at your church, civic organization, or even in your speech class. How many responses do you need? While the answer to this question depends on several factors, a good rule of thumb is to try to get as many responses as you can. For a speech, about one hundred people is a good goal.

Pretest your questions with a few people to see if they understand your directions and questions. Make any changes necessary before you administer the survey to your larger sample group. It's also a good idea to let your instructor check it before distributing it to your group.

Surveys take time to prepare, distribute, and tabulate. Nevertheless, they provide a good way to collect current information. If you can't take time to prepare and conduct a survey, check for surveys that have already been done. A survey can be very helpful if you need to know what people are thinking about a particular topic.

Media

We live in what has been dubbed the Information Age. In addition to the Internet, we have access to information via other *media.* Televisions, radios, DVDs, and CDs are present in practically every home in America. Workplaces often allow employees access to the media, and the commute to and from any destination can be accompanied by the car radio or listening to podcasts on your Ipod. In fact most Americans owe a great deal of what they know to the evening news or to *Oprah.* Although, not all of what is broadcast is correct, information you obtain from these sources, if checked with another source, can provide useful support for your speech.

Many interesting and creative approaches to speeches we have heard have involved music, actual recordings of news events, quotes, or vocal dramatizations. It is one thing to read about a certain type of music, but quite another to hear the actual music. Think about how powerful it would be to listen to an announcer describe an actual event as it takes place. In the past we would have needed to know in advance when such an event was taking place and make arrangements to tape it on our VCRs (where did I put that blank tape?). (Do they still sell them!) Today, TV and radio shows have searchable databases on their Web sites that can quickly provide you with these kinds of sources without you having to worry about recording anything.

Illustrations

We often hear the phrase, "seeing is believing." What better way to explain or prove a point than to show your audience what you are talking about? You could talk about how devastating it is to rebuild after a natural disaster, but it is even more effective to show illustrations of the damage done in a flood, hurricane, or tornado. Projecting such images has become relatively easy to do as many places have a computer with Internet connection and an attached projector.

Museums and Other Centers

If you live near a metropolitan area, the city is full of places to do research and have fun at the same time. Museums dedicated to art, history, and thousands of other topics are tucked away in cities all over the country. Even smaller towns have museums that can be used for research purposes. Science centers are interactive and provide data on all sorts of topics. Zoos and aquariums are filled with information about animals and aquatic life. All these places can provide you with useful material for your speeches. Find out the names and addresses of the sources that are relevant to your speech and visit or write to them for information. You can even "visit" many of these places in cyberspace via the Internet. Take a virtual tour to gain useful data.

Organizations and Businesses

There are local, regional, national, and international organizations and businesses dedicated to the pursuit and distribution of information on just about any topic. These groups usually publish newsletters, pamphlets, or brochures about their area of interest and expertise. Frequently they can provide up-to-date information that may be difficult to find elsewhere. They often have a Web site that is full of valuable data. If you don't know the names of organizations that would be useful in your search, go to the library and find the *Encyclopedia of Associations* or the *Directory of Nonprofit Organizations* (also available online). These directories will list addresses, Web sites and telephone numbers. A word of caution is necessary about information you may obtain from these companies or organizations. These groups have a personal stake in their subject, therefore, the information you receive may be biased and should not be used as your only source. Statistics and facts should be verified with other sources if for no other reason than to help you establish credibility with your audience.

The Library

Remember that place with all the books? Don't forget the advantages that a library can provide. The reason a library exists is to provide multiple sources of information at one convenient location. Libraries are very user-friendly and librarians are knowledgeable people who are there to assist you. If you don't know where to start or are having difficulties, ask the librarian. Just don't expect him or her to do your research for you; that's your job.

Researching is easier if you are familiar with the facilities you will be using. Most libraries offer an orientation or tour of their holdings, information on how to use the computerized databases, and tutorials on using other electronic sources. If your school offers such help, take advantage of this opportunity. You will be surprised at the different sources available. Every library is different, but here we list the most commonly used library sources.

The *library catalog* is one of the most familiar and well-used sources in the library. Here you will find listed all the sources your library has available. Using your library's computerized catalog is very similar to using a search engine on the Internet. Most card catalogs are divided into three sections according to subject, author, or title. Usually, you will find that looking under the subject heading will be the easiest and quickest way to use the catalog. Once you've found the books you believe you need, look at the numbers and letters of the data entry. They refer to the system your library uses to organize

The library is a great place for locating books and other resource materials for a speech topic, including journals, magazines, and newspapers. Most libraries also have computers that the public can use.

material, and will show you the location of your book. You can locate the section your book is in by matching the letters and numbers that appear on the computer screen to the corresponding notation on the stacks (bookshelves).

Reference works are materials such as encyclopedias, *The World Almanac, Who's Who in America,* dictionaries, and texts that include information about specific topics. These will be listed in the library catalog and can be found the same way you find other books. You can also look for the reference section in your library and browse. Browsing allows you to look around. You will be surprised at the different sources you can find.

Books and encyclopedias are excellent sources of basic general knowledge. However, you should be aware that because of the time it takes to publish any given book, the information contained therein is probably one to two years old, despite the copyright date. Do not assume that just because you have a book whose copyright date is this year, you have current information on that topic. To find the most current material, periodicals are your best source.

Periodicals are magazines, newspapers, and journals (found in print or online). These will usually be in a specific section of the library devoted only to them or available at the library's computer stations. You will also find that many of these works (particularly newspapers) have been transferred to microfilm or are available digitally.

If this is the case, consult the librarian for assistance in accessing the material. To find particular articles about your topic, you will want to refer to the abstracts and indexes. For popular magazines you will probably use *The Readers' Guide to Periodical Literature.* For more specific, specialized areas, you should look at other indexes that contain references to your topic. Most national professional journals are titled *The Journal of the American . . . , The American . . . ,* or *National Society of . . . ,* so remember to look under National, American, or Journal when using an index to search for sources. The best way to use these guides is to look under several general headings that may contain your topic. This will help you locate articles that relate to your topic, which you can then look up.

Don't limit yourself to the use of a single library. Unless you live in an isolated area, you should have access to several libraries. Even if you can't check out materials from each library, you can still probably do research there. Most libraries are partners with other libraries. Users of one library can request books from another through interlibrary loans. Remember that if you make this type of request, it may take up to a week before you receive the materials you requested, so plan ahead. Electronic databases the library subscribes to can provide data from other locations that can be accessed and downloaded immediately. You may be able to find much of what you need using the library.

How Do You Choose the Best Source?

While your research plan should have helped you decide what types of support you need for your speech, and we have examined the various sources

available to find that support, you still need to consider what you will actually include in your speech. What information will be the most effective in
helping to establish your credibility? What will interest your audience and
substantiate what you say? In comparing information that we have found in
numerous articles, textbooks, and research, we believe that there are five
things you should consider when deciding what research to use in a speech.

1. *Proximity.* Recent examples, events, quotes, or occurrences are more
   credible. The exception to this is when referring to a historical event.
   Using support that considers timeliness also helps gain and maintain
   attention, which aids in comprehension and understanding. Choosing
   current examples and recent sources should be a consideration in
   choosing your material.

2. *Relevancy.* Information that corresponds directly to your topic and
   audience is the most effective. The supportive material you incorporate in your speech should be applicable to both. This allows your listeners to make the connection between what you say and their own
   lives for maximum effectiveness.

3. *Significance.* When choosing information, consider its significance to
   your topic and purpose. Don't use something because it was the first
   support you found. The material should be relevant (see #2) and
   should support the points of your speech. Don't use abstract examples.
   You need to explain terms and include specific examples that provide
   a definition. For example, you might explain how the fact that not voting in an election could be considered unpatriotic. This would help
   your audience understand the significance of what behavior would be
   considered patriotic, rather than defining the word patriotism.

4. *Variety.* Use many different kinds of support. Use examples, quotations, statistics, and visual/audio aids in your speech. Using a variety
   of support material is of more interest to your audience. Some members of the audience may relate well to facts while others would better
   understand your topic if you supply a visual example.

5. *Suitability.* Material that is inappropriate can defeat your purpose if
   used in your speech. Judging the suitability of material shouldn't be
   difficult. By considering your audience, the event, and any directions
   you have been given by your instructor or the person who requested
   that you speak, you can avoid defensive reactions from your audience.
   Consider your audience and don't speak above or below them. Avoid
   material that requires knowledge of specific jargon (terms known only
   by those involved in the topic). Define any terms you are using so that
   the audience can relate to the material.

How do you know that the references, examples, and sources you have
now chosen are reliable and credible? Your credibility as a speaker is a signif-

icant factor in delivering an effective speech, and *your* credibility relies primarily upon the credibility of your sources.

How do you ensure your sources are credible?

Doing a credibility check is as simple as A, B, C, D.

Consider the following information when determining if a source is reliable:

Authority—Author whose experience or knowledge qualifies him or her as a valid source of information.

Bias—Implied or stated political or ideological preferences?

Content/Currency—Breadth and depth of the material supplied, quality of writing, age of information.

Design—Layout and user-friendliness of a Web site.

Here is a more thorough checklist for evaluating information when using the ABCD model.

1. Authority

- Who is providing the information?
- Is a specific author cited for the works?
- Are the author's credentials/biographical information provided?
- Is the author known in his or her field of expertise?
- Do you recognize the author's name or works from other sources?
- If online, were you linked to the site from a Web site you consider reliable?
- Who is the publisher (organization, commercial site, academic)?
- Is the publisher a reliable, well-known source?
- Is the publisher a suitable resource for your topic and audience?
- If an Internet site, is the domain an educational (.edu), nonprofit organization (.org), or a government site (.gov)? These are often more reliable than commercial (.com) sites.
- Are the author's sources cited?

2. Bias

- Can you detect any preference for political or ideological beliefs?
- Is the purpose of the paper, Web site, or other source of information clearly stated?
- Who appears to be the target audience for the material?

- If a Web site, is it a .com (commercial site) whose purpose is to sell something?
- What are the goals or guidelines of the organization?
- Are many viewpoints represented?
- Are opinions presented as fact or supported with fact?

3. **Content/Currency**
   - Does the source provide a well-rounded overview of the subject?
   - What level of detail is provided?
   - Does the source provide verifiable facts?
   - Are opinions of the author or publisher clearly labeled as opinions?
   - What data or references are provided for verification?
   - What's the quality of the writing?
   - Are there frequent errors in grammar, spelling, or sentence construction?
   - How much information is given?
   - How old is the information provided?
   - Has it been updated recently?

4. **Design (primarily a consideration for Web sites)**
   - Is the Web site attractive?
   - Is the Web site easy to navigate?
   - Is there a recognizable logo or masthead that indicates the site is actually part of another reputable site (like a college)?
   - Is the look glitzy but the information scanty?
   - Can you contact the Web master or content owner?
   - Can you find the information you need to verify ABC (authority, bias, content)?
   - Has the site won any awards?
   - Has the site been reviewed by other publications?
   - If reviewed, what do the reviews say?

Establishing credibility means you need to be very judicious about trusting the validity of the information you obtain, especially from Web sites. You need to make sure all your sources are reliable and credible. That may take a little extra work for Internet sources. Therefore we would like to take a moment to discuss wiki software.

A *wiki* is simply a software program (much like any other word-processing program) that allows for quick and easy collaboration in creating and writing a document. There are numerous sites available where you can create a wiki and then invite others to access, add, delete, and edit "the paper." This technology is very useful for those projects that you need to accomplish in collaboration with others (a report for work or a group project for a class assignment). However, its greatest asset (multiple people being able to edit a document) is also its greatest liability. How do you know that what is contained in the document is factual and credible? If you are using a wiki to collaborate on a report, there isn't much problem. But, if you are using a wiki document as a source for your speech, there could be a real problem.

If you use the Internet at all, you are probably familiar with Wikipedia. As the name implies, this is an online encyclopedia that uses wiki software. Students love to use Wikipedia for sources. Your authors understand the lure and admit to checking out information at the site when we are doing our own research. It's very user friendly and there are thousands of hyperlinks that add layers of data to a search with just a keystroke. Be careful using this as a source. Why? Because contributors to Wikipedia can be anyone and the information they post may or may not be true. Wikipedia does have guidelines and the vast majority of the material posted is done so by those who are knowledgeable. The problem is, it can be edited by anyone. During the 2008 presidential primary campaigns, Wikipedia was misused to disperse inaccurate information about all three candidates. Barack Obama's data was edited to say he is a Muslim, Hillary Clinton was misquoted, and John McCain's birth date was changed to make it appear he was older than he actually is.

Strengthen Your Skills

Scavenger Hunt

Purpose: To give you experience finding credible sources to support your speech points.

Procedure: Use the Internet or the library to find a source that gives you the answers to these questions. Explain why you believe the source to be credible.

1. When and where was the first performance of Bizet's *Carmen*?
2. What does *mellifluous* mean?
3. Who was Isak Dinesen?
4. Where is the Jutland Peninsula located?
5. Who was Felix Frankfurter?
6. What is the most famous song written by Irving Berlin?
7. In what month and year did the Phoenix Mars Mission locate ice on Mars?
8. How tall is the Eiffel Tower without its antenna?
9. How many home runs did Cardinal Mark McGuire hit in 1998?
10. What actor originally played Albus Dumbledore in the Harry Potter films?

The site was locked down for a few hours to make corrections. However, there is simply too much data to consistently review 24/7, so when using Wikipedia, check the information you find with another source before using it as support in your speech.

When you begin researching sources, don't leave your common sense behind. Ask yourself how accurate you think the information you have found is, by using the ABCD checklist. Remember the effectiveness of your speech depends on your credibility as a speaker. Your credibility depends on the credibility of your sources.

How Much Research Is Enough?

How do you know when you've done enough research? How much support is actually needed for a speech? For major research projects, the rule is to continue your search until you no longer find "new" information. For speeches you will be giving in class and most other situations, we can modify that exhaustive rule. You will need at least one source to serve as your primary source. This source should be fairly comprehensive, current, and cover your general topic. Additional sources should be used as needed.

You will always do more research than you will use. The more you investigate, the more confident you will be at the podium. As an added bonus, you will be better prepared to address questions from the audience if they arise.

Conclusion

Let's face it, if you want to do something well, you need to dedicate an appropriate amount of time to preparation. An effective speech requires time to prepare. Researching is part of that step. You can be better prepared and use your time more effectively if you make a research plan and take research notes. Remember the sources you choose to support your speech topic need to be credible and reliable. It's not hard to find sources for your topic. The catch is to locate the best sources for your work.

Application to Everyday Life

Because we live in a country that allows freedom of speech, we are often bombarded by other people's opinions, interpretations, and perceptions as they exercise their constitutional rights. However, it may not always be in our best interest to believe, trust, or apply all of these messages. How do you know if a salesperson is trying to sell you merchandise you don't need, that is inferior to the competition's, or that is overpriced? How do you know if a political ad actually reflects the candidate's voting record or if it is a distortion by the opposition to gain votes? How do you know if an e-mail message is true or just an Internet myth? Has it been digitally edited? The answer is, do your research, apply a credibility check, and then make educated decisions. The ABCD model can be applied to many situations in your day-to-day life.

DISCUSSION QUESTIONS

1. In what ways will "Proper Planning Prevent Poor Performance" help you be a more effective speaker?
2. Choose a topic and list several sources you could use that you already know exist.
3. What are four sources not found in the library or on the Internet that can be used to research your topic?
4. What considerations should you use when choosing sources to support your topic?
5. Why do you need to use the ABCD model to check the credibility of your sources, especially those found on the Internet?

KEY WORDS

- authority
- bias
- content
- currency
- design
- Internet
- Internet address
- interview
- library catalog
- media
- periodicals
- personal experience
- plagiarism
- proximity
- reference works
- relevancy
- research
- research plan
- significance
- suitability
- surveys
- variety
- wiki

9

Get It in Writing!

Preparing Research Notes and the Bibliography

- Research notes can help you organize your research.
- There are seven steps to taking good research notes.
- Keep a record of your sources for your bibliography.
- A formal bibliography must conform to an acceptable format.

Pam has just looked over some notes Barry Foster has prepared after doing some research on the new computer software program the company is adopting. She isn't sure why he wanted her to review them. After all, he is the only one that will see them or that can understand them. She is not sure what all the little letters and numbers in the corners mean either. She hopes he does! One thing Pam is going to suggest is that Barry prepare a list of references that he can give to employees in case they want to do some additional research on their own. Besides, you never know when someone will ask where your information came from, or if he or she will want to do research independently. It is always best to keep a record and be prepared!

Now that you understand how important it is to research your topic for your speech, we'd like to offer some guidelines for preparing your research notes and your bibliography. Using the following information will help you prepare a record of the work you have done to find support for your speech.

Research Notes

Once you have found the sources you want, you must have a way of recording the information you plan on using in your speech. This is true no matter where your material comes from: printed sources, interviews, or any other media. Your authors realize that many of you print out sources from the Internet or make copies of printed material. Armed with your pile of papers, you then start highlighting or underlining the information you want to use. We suggest that you add a step to that process and create *research notes*.

Many of you are already proficient in note taking. You may have already developed your own style—something that works well for you. If this is true, then the following information should not affect your current method. If, however, you don't know how to take notes, have difficulty organizing notes, or have trouble deciphering what you've written, then the following suggestions will help you become a more efficient note taker in many situations. Research notes are not the notes you will be taking with you to the podium. These notes are for organizing your research only. There are seven steps to taking good research notes.

It's easy to accumulate information from many different sources. Therefore, research notes can help you keep track of your sources and create a bibliography.

1. **Locate all the sources you plan to use for your speech.** If there are many references for your topic, keep only the most comprehensive or up-to-date sources. An overabundance of materials will complicate your research. Once you have chosen those that you will actually use, move on to the next step.

2. **Choose one primary source.** Use the source that you believe is the most comprehensive as your *primary source* of information. The notes on this reference will be the most thorough.

3. **Decide what pertinent information you need from your other sources.** Since you will be taking basic information from your primary source, your other sources must do one or more of the following to be *pertinent information.*

   a. Provide additional support for your primary source.

   b. Fill in information missing from the primary source.

   c. Give a more detailed account than the primary source does.

   d. Approach the information in a creative or different way.

   e. Enhance the topic with audio/visual aids, examples, or other means of support or explanation.

4. **Gather all your sources together.** If it is possible to have all your sources available in one spot, do so. This will save time and be less confusing.

5. **Use note cards to record your notes.** Using note cards (ruled or unruled, any size) will enable you to categorize and locate your various bits of information more easily than searching through sheets of notebook paper or hard copies of Web pages. You can label each note card, and divide them into categories.

6. **Make bibliography cards for all your sources.** For each source, make a separate *bibliography card* that contains the necessary information for citing it as a source in your bibliography. (Standard bibliography form is covered in the next section of this chapter.) When you have recorded all your sources, label each source card with a capital A, B, C, etc., in the upper right hand corner of the card. Your first source would be A, your second B, etc.

7. **Make notes on each source.** Now you are ready to begin taking notes on your topic. Each note card should be labeled by the capital letter assigned to the reference it is taken from and numbered chronologically, for example, the first card from source A would be marked "A1," the second "A2," and so on. By labeling your notes, you will know what source they are from and in what order they were recorded. Give each note a heading, describing what the information on the card is about. For instance, if the information is historical background on your topic label the card as such. Put only information about that heading on that card. Do not combine information, or sorting it out later will be difficult.

If you decide to use a direct quotation, put quotation marks around it and note the page number where it appeared so you can include it in your bibliography. This will also serve as a reminder to you to state your source during your speech in order to avoid plagiarism. Paraphrased notes may be written in complete sentences or phrases; it doesn't matter as long as you can understand them when you need them later. Take notes on anything you think you will need to illustrate or explain your topic. If you stick to your research plan, you won't be distracted by extraneous information.

When you have taken all your notes, you should organize the bibliography. You can add it to your outline later.

How to Prepare a Bibliography

The last step is preparing the *bibliography.* If your research and note taking have been done accurately, you should have no trouble completing this step.

Your bibliography is a list of the sources you used to prepare your speech. You need to alphabetize the cards you have already made of your sources. If you have conducted interviews, you should make a card for each of them as well. Some bibliographies are separated into "printed" and "non-printed" sources. Check with your instructor about the form he or she requires. Alphabetizing occurs by the last name of the author or the first significant word of the title (if no author is given), or the last name of the interviewed party.

The form for bibliographies is standard, and the bibliography should follow the conclusion section of your formal outline. It is necessary that you give credit to any source you used in the preparation of your speech and also cite them orally during your delivery. The following information shows the standard procedure for listing frequently used sources. Should you need to include any other type of reference, please refer to any standard writing text or go online and search for MLA. English Department Faculty are also a good source for this information. There are even sites that will format a bibliography for you.

Strengthen Your Skills

Go Surfing

Purpose: Find a credible Web site that will format your bibliography in standard format for you.

Procedure:

1. Use your favorite search engine to find a Web site that will format bibliographic information into a standard format.

2. Use the ABCD method (in the previous chapter) to determine if your site is credible.

3. If you determine it is a credible site, go to step 4. If you cannot determine its credibility, start over at step 1.

4. Enter the bibliography information required for a book (by two authors) using this text as the source.

5. Keep a record of this site in case you need to use it in the future.

Please note the following format is MLA style; you may also use APA style or any other standard acceptable form. Check with your instructor to see if he or she has a preference.

Books
Last, First name of author. <u>Title of Book.</u> Publisher's location: Publisher, year published.

Book with More Than One Author
Last, First, and First Last names of authors. <u>Title of Book</u>. Publisher's location: Publisher, year published.

Book by a Corporate or Organization Author
Name of corporation or organization. <u>Title of Book</u>. Publisher's location: Publisher, year published.

Poem or Short Story Example
Last, First name of author. "Title of Poem or Short Story." Publisher's location: Publisher, year published. Page number.

Article in Reference Book
"Title of Article." <u>Name of Reference Book</u>. Year published.

The Bible
<u>Title of Bible</u>. Last, First name of editor, gen. ed. Publisher's location: Publisher, year published.

A Government Publication
Country publishing. Branch of government (committee if available). <u>Title of Publication</u>. number and session if available. Location of Publisher: Publisher, year published.

A Pamphlet
<u>Title of Pamphlet</u>. Location of Publisher or organization: Name of publisher or organization, year published.

Article in a Magazine
Last, First name of author. "Title of Article." <u>Title of Magazine</u> day Month year: page(s).

Article in a Newspaper
Last, First name of author. "Title of Article." <u>Name of Newspaper</u> [city, state]. day Month year: page.

Editorial
"Title of Editorial." Editorial. <u>Name of Paper or Magazine</u> (edition if applicable). day Month year: page number.

Article in a Scholarly Journal
Last, First name of authors. "Title of Article." <u>Title of Journal</u>. Volume number. Issue (and/or year): pages.

Personal or Telephone Interview (also use for Personal Experience citation)
Last, First name of person interviewed. Personal Interview. day Month year.

Lecture or Speech

Last, First name of speaker. Type of Speech. Title or topic of speech. Location of speech (e.g., Marriott Hotel or University of Illinois). City where speech given, state. day Month year.

Painting, Sculpture, or Photograph

Last, First name of artist. Name of Art. Name of Institution that houses the work, City.

Broadcast Television or Radio Program

"Title of episode." Title of Show. Network name. Call letters and City of local station. day Month year.

Recorded Television Shows

"Title of episode." Title of Recording. List Writers. List Director. Network. Episode original airing date day month year. Type of recording (i.e., DVD, VHS). Studio, year released.

Entire Sound Recording

Last, First name of artist (or Group). Title of Recording. Recording Company, year.

Individual Songs

Last, First name of artist (or Group). "Title of Song." Album. Recording Company, year.

Movies in Theaters

Title of Movie. Director's name. Main Performers names. Studio/Production Company, year.

Recorded Movies

Title of Movie. Director's name. Main Performers names. Year originally released. Type of recording (i.e., DVD, VHS). Distributor, year released as recording.

Advertisement

Company Advertising. Title of Publication ad appears in day Month year: page ad appears on.

A Legal Document

Name of document. Publication Number (identification number). day Month year printed.

A Map or Chart

Title of map (e.g., Washington). Type (e.g., Map, Chart). City, State printed: Source (e.g., Washington Department of Transportation), year.

A Cartoon or Comic Strip

Last, First name of artist. "Title of Comic or Cartoon." Type (i.e., Comic Strip, Political Cartoon). Title of Publication source appears in [City of publication] day Month year: page

(continued)

A Letter or Memo
Last, First name of author. "Title" (if one). day Month year. Letter abc or Title of Collection. Editor (if one). Company/Institution. City, State of company/institution: day Month year. page numbers.

Class/Lecture Notes Taken By Student
In a lecture on date, in name of class, Name of professor stated, "your quotation or note."

Class/Lecture Notes Distributed by Professor
Last, First name of Professor. "Title/Topic of Presentation." Type of notes (i.e., Class notes, PowerPoint presentation). Name of Class, Institution. day Month year.

Web Sources
You will not always be able to find all the information a Web site should provide, but always try to find as much as you can. Include:

- The author, editor, corporation, or organization
- Name or title of project, book, article
- Date of version, revision, or posting
- Publisher information
- Date you accessed the material
- URL (Web address)

An Entire Web Site
Name of Site. Date of Posting/Revision. Name of institution/organization affiliated with the site (sometimes found in copyright statements). Date you accessed the site [URL electronic address].

A Page on a Web Site
"Title of Page" Name of Web Site. Date Posted by source. Date accessed by you. [URL electronic address].

An Image, Including a Video, Painting, Sculpture, or Photograph Online
Last, First name of artist. Name of Art. Year created. Location of Art, Country. Date accessed by you. [URL electronic address].

An Article in a Web Magazine
Last, First Name of author. "Title of Article." Title of Publication. Date of publication. Date accessed by you. [URL electronic address].

E-mail or Other Personal Communication
Last, First name of author. "Subject/Title of message" (if any). Name of person who received e-mail. Date message sent.

A Listserv or E-mail Discussion List Posting
Last, First name of author (maybe screen name). "Title of Posting." Type of Posting. Date when material was posted. Name of listserv. Date accessed by you. [URL electronic address].

Discussion Board/Forum Posting
Screen name of poster. "Title/Subject of posting" Online posting date.
   Date posted. Date accessed by you. [URL electronic address].

Blog Postings
Last, First name of blogger (or screen name) "Title of Entry." Weblog
   Entry. Title of Weblog. Date Posted. Date accessed by you. [URL
   electronic address].

For Notes Available Online as PDFs and PowerPoint Slides on Course Site
Last, First name of instructor. "Title of Document." Type of notes
   (Class notes, PowerPoint). Date uploaded (or created, if known).
   Course title. Course home page. Department, Institution. Date
   accessed by you. [URL electronic address].

Conclusion

Researching can be time-consuming whether done online or in the
library. Do yourself a favor and maximize your productivity when you
research by following the guidelines provided here. They will help you keep
track of important useful information and save time. Remember that you will
need to cite (state) your sources orally in your speech as you refer to them,
but you also need to cite them correctly (standard bibliography form) on
your outline.

Application to Everyday Life

We all find ourselves in discussions with others on a daily basis. Many of these
conversations include the sharing of personal opinions about various topics. In
order to strengthen our "argument" we often will quote or cite something we
have heard in the media or read online. Usually we remark, "They say . . ." Well,
as my grandfather used to always ask, "Who is they?" Being able to explain
what your source is adds a great deal of credibility to your part of the discussion. Consider stating your sources in your everyday conversations.

DISCUSSION QUESTIONS

1. How might the method of taking research notes presented in this chapter save you time from your present method?
2. How do research notes differ from speaking notes?
3. What does "standard bibliography form" mean?
4. Why do you need to list more than the URL for Internet sources?
5. What information do you need to cite a blog posting?

KEY WORDS

- bibliography
- bibliography cards
- pertinent information
- primary source
- research notes

10

Almost Showtime!

Final Preparations

- Audio/visual aids are an important element that can enhance your speech.
- There are numerous types of these aids that you can use to enhance your presentations.
- Digital presentations can help you create effective audio/visual aids.
- There are a few simple rules to apply to any aid you use.
- After considering your audio/visual aids, you are ready to create your speech notes.
- The final notes you take to the podium are very important.
- They should be in order and numbered.
- The old saying "practice makes perfect" is certainly applicable to public speaking.
- Practicing provides you an opportunity to make adjustments to your speech.

John is meeting with all of the speakers in the auditorium today. The conference is still two weeks away, but the speakers are ready to deliver their speech. They are meeting today to practice with the digital presentation media and software as well as practice with the microphone. John has also asked the maintenance crew to be on hand to adjust the lighting as well. John is not sure how long the practice session will take. He knows from past experience that he always like to go over his presentations several times before the actual presentation. He had better call home. It may be a late night!

All the work you have done so far has prepared you to know what you are going to speak about, the people you will be speaking to, the reason for your speech, what you will actually say, and where your speech will take place. You may believe that you are ready to present your speech. But remember you are not handing the audience a written report. You will be speaking aloud to people who will not only be listening to you, but watching you as well. Although it sounds time-consuming, delivery is actually the least time-consuming of your preparation steps. However, before you can deliver your speech you must decide what additional elements you could use to enhance your speech, prepare your speaking notes, and then take time to practice!

Audio/Visual Aids

Beginning speakers often overlook a very important element that can enhance their speeches. *Audio/visual aids* can help you get your message across to your audience and help you keep their interest. They can also help you with speech anxiety by giving you an additional element on which to focus your energy.

Audio/visual aids are elements that assist speakers in communicating their message. There are numerous types of aids that can be used to enhance your presentation. Objects (like a souvenir from a vacation), a video on You-Tube, or other items can be used to help a speaker present a message.

Why Are They Important?

Your main purpose as a speaker is to deliver specific information to your audience while keeping them interested. Using visual representations or audio clips can help your audience better understand and maintain interest in what you are telling them because it allows them to engage an additional sensory mode. To hear a description of a tarantula is far less powerful than seeing one. You could listen to someone explain jazz, but it is much more exciting to hear a clip of some great New Orleans jazz. You can describe the smell of the ocean breeze on your beach vacation, but adding burning incense or air freshener that smells like that breeze would be more enticing. Allowing your audience to use additional methods, not just hearing, helps them to experience your message fully.

Types

The first thought that probably emerged when you thought about audio/visual aids was a poster. Today we have many more choices for adding elements to enhance our speech delivery. Most college classrooms and almost all speaking engagement sites will have access to computers and projectors. This is one of those factors you should find out about as you determine the physical environment of where you will be speaking. Let's examine the various types of audio/visual aids that you might consider using.

Posters, Flipcharts, and Overhead Projectors

We bet you all had to make a *poster* for some school activity in the past. For those of you who are "crafty," you probably liked making them. For others it was a struggle to make anything. While paper posters may still be used on occasion, they are really a thing of the past. It will be rare that you will be asked to speak in an environment that doesn't have equipment available for digital presentations (remember to check out the facilities before you speak). The good news is that those of you who want to be creative can do it on a computer. You'll even have options you didn't have with your poster board and scissors. The result will look professional if you follow a few rules, which we will discuss later in this chapter. For those of you who dreaded the poster assignment, you, too, can create a professional display by using simple computer software. Just pick a format and background for your "poster" and fill in your information.

A *flipchart* is a big tablet of paper you see propped up on an easel at a meeting. With the addition of a few colored markers a flipchart can serve as an excellent way to brainstorm or keep track of ideas during a meeting. However, since you will be delivering a speech, you need to consider whether or not you will be using verbal responses from your audience during the speech. If not, a flipchart is probably not useful and is unnecessary.

Overhead projectors in the past were those machines that use a transparency to bounce and magnify an image onto a screen. While their days are probably numbered, they still seem to make appearances in academic classrooms and in hotel conference rooms. Essentially they project information that is printed or drawn on a piece of plastic that is then placed on the projector's surface, which is a lens. An enlarged version of the image appears on a screen in front of the room so that everyone in the room can see it. If this is available to you, use it effectively.

Blackboards and Whiteboards

If you are presenting your speech in an environment that has a *blackboard* or *whiteboard* (think classroom), you can use the board to make quick drawings or charts. Notice the word "quick" in that statement. The board should only be used for simple diagrams or examples that are not large or highly detailed. If you have graphs and charts, lists, drawings, and other more detailed visual elements, prepare them in advance, using some other medium, otherwise you risk the chance of looking unprofessional.

Pictures and Videos

Yes, the old adage one picture is worth a thousand words is correct, particularly when it comes to delivering an effective speech. Adding a *picture* or *video* to your explanation helps your audience understand your material by "seeing" it. Talking about someone? Show us a picture of the person; in fact, if your speech is primarily about one person, place or thing, show several pictures. Do you have a short video from YouTube or a clip from a movie? Show it to us. Learn how to create a media presentation and incorporate it into an effective slide show. Few other techniques are as effective for your audience as adding an appropriately placed picture to your speech.

You should not pass a picture around to your audience during your speech. It is distracting and people don't see it at the time you are discussing it, which makes it confusing and takes the focus off of you, the speaker. If you have a picture that is too small to be seen by the entire audience at one time, it will need to be enlarged either as a digital projection or an actual physical enlargement.

Audio Clips

As mentioned before, you can describe a sound in your speech, but it may not be as effective as hearing an *audio clip* from a CD or other digital source. While you can certainly quote Martin Luther King Jr. by saying, "I have a dream . . . ," think of how much more powerful it would be for your audience if they actually heard his magnificent voice booming the message. Trying to adequately describe the difference between Rock and Jazz can make your audience's head spin; instead play the music! Make sure it is cued up and ready to be heard with a flip of a switch or stroke of key. It is distracting to watch a speaker stop the flow of their speech to find the right track or file.

Microphones

While you probably won't be using a *microphone* to deliver your speeches in class, you may find that they are available and necessary in some speaking situations. Microphones are easy to use but most people make them complicated. If you will be using a microphone there are some basics. First, is the microphone stationary or moveable? This will affect how you move your body during the speech. If you are using a mobile microphone you need to know where you can walk and not get feedback. Make sure that sound checks have been made prior to your speech and control the volume. Know where the "on" switch is. Make sure it is in the on position before you begin speaking. Never tap on a mike, and say, "Can you hear me?" or "testing . . . 1 . . . 2 . . . 3"! This is not one of the "grabber" statements we have discussed and is not the way you want to start your speech. If possible, practice your speech using the equipment you will be using on the day of your presentation.

Objects

What's better than a picture? The *object* itself, if easily portable, beats a picture as a visual aid. Within reason actually bringing the real object for presentation in your speech may be a good option. For example, you could show us a picture of that quilt you or your grandma made, but actually showing us the quilt would be more effective. Demonstration speeches often require numerous objects to be used as props to show the audience step by step how to do something. Actually seeing a procedure is more effective than seeing pictures of it or even a video. The object(s) should be easy to transport and store before and after your speech. Consider its weight and size, and be aware of any policies that are in effect about various objects at the location of your speech. At the community college where we teach, weapons of all kinds are

In his speech about the guitar's role in folk music, the speaker uses an "object"—the guitar—as a visual aid and plays the guitar (audio aid) to illustrate one of the points in his speech.

banned from the campus. Consequently, students doing speeches about guns, knives, hunting, or other activities involving a weapon must use a picture, even if the real object would be more effective. You should also consider your audience's "comfort" level with an object. You may be perfectly comfortable handling your pet snake, but will your audience, or instructor, feel at ease with it curling around your arm?

Don't pass an object around to your audience during your speech. It is distracting and people don't see it when you are discussing it, which makes it confusing and takes the focus off of you. If the object is too small to be seen by the entire audience then you have two options. If available, you can use a camera that when focused on the object, will project its image onto a screen. If this technology isn't available, your other option is to have enough samples of the object so that it can be handed out to all your audience members at one time. While this certainly isn't practical in many instances, it could be useful and effective with small inexpensive items. In fact, a demonstration speech on how to make chocolate chip cookies may not be effective unless you have samples for everyone!

Handouts

A *handout* that provides information related to the speech you have just given us is a useful "take away." The audience might like to have a copy of your Angel Food Cake recipe, or a list of useful Web sites providing free coupons. You might want to pass out copies of a chart you referred to during your speech. If you are using a handout during your speech don't pass it out until you want everyone to look at it. Otherwise it can become a distraction. If the handout is to be taken away, then it is best to pass it out at the end of your speech, unless you want the audience to refer to it during various segments of your speech.

Digital Presentations

Digital presentations are currently the most frequently used medium for presenting audio/visual aids. Digital presentations use computers, software, and projectors to display information. We are probably all familiar with Microsoft's PowerPoint presentational software. It's difficult to find a college classroom, boardroom, meeting room, or conference center that isn't equipped for digital presentations. It's doubtful that anyone reading this has never seen such a digital presentation, in fact, many of you have probably created one. If such equipment is available to you, use it. No matter what software the program uses (PowerPoint is the most commonly used), you'll find it easy to use for producing a quality visual aid to add to your speech delivery. Some presentations are boring and poorly designed. There are some guidelines for digital presentations to help you create an effective one.

These guidelines should be followed when creating a digital slide or slide show. Many of them can also be applied to any graphic you are creating, whether digitally or by hand.

1. **Background.** Choose simple backgrounds that won't compete with your material. Use the same background throughout the presentation.

2. **Color.** Black, blue, and green are the most visible. Avoid purple, brown, pink, and yellow. Use no more than four colors overall in your presentation.

3. **Clutter.** Don't put too much on a slide. Leave empty space, it will be easier for your audience to understand the words and graphics.

4. **Fonts.** Use sans-serif fonts (without the little "hooks") such as Arial or Helvetica, as they are easier on the eyes than serif fonts such as Times New Roman or Palatino. Use an 18- to 24-point font size or larger for headings. Use the same font throughout the text and avoid using all capital letters.

5. **Graphics.** Include pictures in your presentation. Use them for a reason, not just for decoration. Avoid the use of animation. It is distracting. Use simple electronic transitions and be consistent.

6. **Brief.** Keep the text short and simple. Avoid the use of full sentences and use bullet points. Limit the number of slides. Don't pad the presentation. No one stays interested in a "never ending" slide show.

7. **Charts and graphs should "speak" alone.** Don't add a lot of words to charts or graphs. Create them wisely and let them "speak for themselves." You can refer to them or offer explanations verbally to help the audience follow them.

8. **Imbed.** Imbed your visuals and audio clips into the slides. It makes your speech flow better and you don't waste time setting up multiple files. They are just a click away—easy to access and easy to follow.

9. **Avoid the familiar.** PowerPoint software is commonly used for digital presentations, so your audience may have already seen the clipart and backgrounds. Try to avoid those that are too common and familiar. If you remember them from another presentation, your audience will too. Incorporate your own visuals whenever possible. This will help keep the audience's interest.

10. **Practice.** Use the presentation while you practice your speech. You can learn when to advance the slides and what you need to say. This will decrease your anxiety and relieve your nerves as you learn how to work your way through the presentation *before* you give it!

Now that we have discussed the various types of audio/visual aids you can use to enhance your presentation, we will discuss some additional things you should consider. There are a few simple rules you should apply to any and all aids you are using during your speech. They should all be:

- **Brief.** Aids add interest, they should be short and to the point.
- **Discernable.** They should be easy to see, hear, taste, touch, or smell.
- **Manageable.** Know how to manage and use your equipment.
- **Appropriate.** For you, them, the occasion, and the location.
- **Properly placed.** An aid needs to be used in a specific section of your speech and then removed.
- **Used.** As our colleague Jeff Harrison says, "Aids are not set dressing."
- **Ignored.** Do not talk to your visual aid. You can point from the side, but never face your aid. Never deliver your speech with your back to your audience.

Follow the simple rules above, and you'll be rewarded with an attentive audience.

Speech Notes

Now that you have an outline for your speech and have chosen the audio/visual elements to enhance your delivery, you should begin preparing the notes you will use to practice your speech. This may be the first of several sets of *speech notes,* as you may adjust them each time you practice. Strive for improvement each time as the final notes you take with you to the podium are very important. Make the notes simple and brief. Typical 3 x 5 note cards are rather small to use for speech notes, since you should be able to quickly glance at your notes without losing your train of thought. Four by six note cards tend to be a more usable size. You can use 8 x 12 sheets of paper, but the length makes it more difficult to find your next point easily. Keep in mind that several sheets of paper may rustle if sorted and become a distraction.

Be sure to have your notes in the proper order and, if they aren't bound, number each card to keep them sequential. Make sure they are neat and legible. Don't try to fit everything on just a few note cards. The purpose of podium notes is to allow you to view your points at a glance. Too much writing on one card makes it difficult to focus. Many speakers choose to use their outline as podium notes. In fact, this is the choice of most professional speakers as well as your authors when they lecture. Your notes are personal and should work for you. They are your lifeline if your thoughts fail at the podium. Guard them—they are gold! Now that you have your podium notes compiled, it is time to use them to practice your speech.

Practice

The old saying *"practice makes perfect"* is certainly applicable to public speaking. You can gain valuable insight from practicing that will provide you with the information you need to make adjustments to your speech before you present it to your audience. Practice giving your speech to another person, use a recorder or camcorder, or watch yourself in a full-length mirror. By doing one or all of these things, several times, you can find out how you will look and sound to your audience.

Although you won't know exactly what you will do at the podium when you actually deliver your speech, practicing it will reveal if any adjustments need to be made. Practicing can also help you to determine how long your presentation will take to deliver. Through practice you can gain mastery over your volume, pitch, and speaking rate, as well as the time element of your speech. You can discover if you overuse "um" and "uh." You will learn about your eye contact, gesturing, and appearance. Practice using your audio/visual aids. Be sure to note any adjustments that are needed in your final notes. Without rehearsal, your speech won't be effective—practice is important.

Conclusion

The actual delivery of your speech depends on preparation and practice. This step is just as important as preparing the content of your speech. If your presentation doesn't keep the audience interested, it doesn't matter what words you use. An effective speaker will use audio/visual aids to add interest and comprehension. You'll be able to approach the podium with your final speech notes and know you can do a good job. After all, practice really can make perfect.

Application to Everyday Life

We are surrounded by audio/visual aids in our daily lives. Most people are at least partially visual learners and understand most easily when something is seen. We use maps to get directions to a location so we can find our destination. We show people pictures of our families and take pictures on vacations to remember our experiences and share them with others. We listen to the radio or music almost constantly in our cars and share our choices of music with others. Enhancing what we say by adding visual and audio elements helps people grasp our ideas.

DISCUSSION QUESTIONS

1. What is the advantage of using audio/visual aids?
2. What are some disadvantages of using photographs in a speech?
3. Why are your final notes so important?
4. Why is practicing your speech important for an effective delivery?
5. What should you look or listen for when practicing your speech?

KEY WORDS

- audio clip
- audio/visual aids
- blackboard
- digital presentations
- flipchart
- handout
- microphone
- object
- overhead projector
- picture
- poster
- practice
- speech notes
- video
- whiteboard

11

Time to Shine

Delivery

Chapter Highlights

- Delivery is the process of actually presenting your speech to an audience.
- There are four ways that speeches can be delivered.
- There are two categories of delivery elements.
- Verbal elements are those that deal with language.
- Language depends on words to convey a message.
- Elements that are not specifically related to language can also enhance what you say to your audience.
- These nonverbal elements are exactly what the word implies, *not verbal*. They are *not* language.
- A question and answer period is often a standard feature in most speaking engagements.

Today's the day! John and Pam are helping the speakers with last-minute preparations before the actual conference begins. The speakers have practiced their speeches numerous times. They are comfortable with their information and are knowledgeable enough to deal with questions from the audience with ease. They all sounded very interesting during their practice sessions and their voices were smooth and clear. Each presenter is dressed in attire with the company's logo, and they all look very professional. John checked and double-checked all of the equipment this morning, and Pam checked the lights. All of the employees are in their assigned seats and ready to begin. Pam has lined up the speakers backstage and they are all aware of when they are expected to speak. John has signaled Pam that it is time to begin. The Director of Public Relations volunteered to do the Welcome Speech and is now approaching the podium. Here they go, time for the show!

This is what it has all been leading up to. It's your time to shine at the podium. All the hard work of focusing, researching, and organizing has prepared you and put the finishing touches on your speech. Now get ready to stand and deliver!

Delivery: What Is It and Why Is It Important?

Delivery is the process of presenting your speech to an audience. It is accomplished through the use of verbal and nonverbal elements of communication. Language or the words you say are the verbal elements of delivery. Anything that is not language, such as facial expressions and gestures, are examples of nonverbal elements of delivery. All of these factors have a significant impact on the effectiveness of your delivery.

You may believe that the information you have gathered to share with your audience is the most important part of your speech. Certainly the content is a major factor in how effectively you will communicate with your audience. However, the way you deliver your message is equally important. In fact, without an effective delivery, your audience may drift off. They may never hear the information you have spent so much time researching and organizing. This makes delivery a key factor in becoming an effective communicator.

Your delivery must complement and reinforce your content, not contradict it. Picture two speakers: both are trying to convince you that their political candidate is the one you should vote for; both have facts to support their contentions and you are an undecided voter. The first person speaks softly in a monotone, using no gestures (except to scratch her nose), and her only other movement is a slight swaying from side to side. An election poster with the candidate's picture and slogan is hanging behind her. She stares at the audience with a blank look throughout her speech. Our second speaker projects her voice so that she can be heard and her vocal fluctuations make her words "come alive." Gestures emphasize her message and her face reflects that she believes every word she is saying. Her speech is supported with a media presentation that includes pictures, graphs, charts, and even music and voice clips of the candidate.

Which speaker are you most likely to listen to and believe? Who is giving her candidate the most "bang for his buck"? Can you see how important delivery is in relaying a message to an audience? Let's see how we can achieve a delivery that emphasizes the content you've prepared in a manner that the audience will find interesting and easy to listen too.

Types of Delivery

There are four ways that speeches can be delivered. The type of delivery you choose depends on the environment in which you will deliver your speech. Choosing the most effective type for your speaking situation is one of the factors that must be considered as part of delivery.

Impromptu

The most common speech is the *impromptu speech*—a spontaneous, unprepared speech usually given without prior notice. This is the kind of speaking we engage in daily. Someone stops us and asks directions. Our boss surprises us with an award at a corporate dinner and asks us to "say a few words." The person who is supposed to introduce your luncheon speaker isn't coming so you have to do the introduction. You are leaving for a weekend and your spouse needs to know the kids' schedule while you are gone. All of these are examples of impromptu speeches.

There are lots of advantages to becoming an effective impromptu speaker. Since it is the type of communication we use most frequently, the better we do it the easier it will be for us to get our message across. Most speech teachers, including us, hope their students will become better impromptu speakers, thus improving their overall communication. However there are disadvantages to impromptu speaking as well. First and foremost, there is no time to prepare. How many of us have experienced a situation where we wish we hadn't said what we did? The best way to become a more effective impromptu speaker is to learn the basics. Having time to prepare, organize, and practice other speeches will more readily prepare you for those situations when you have to think and speak "on your feet." Completing a formal public speaking class is one way to achieve that goal.

Manuscript

If you have ever seen a televised presidential address, you've seen a *manuscript delivery.* Put simply, a manuscript speech is one where the speaker reads, either from a paper text or off a teleprompter. This form of delivery is usually the least effective style in most speaking situations. Those who read their speeches usually have poor delivery skills. Reading causes a speaker to avoid looking at the audience and it also causes them to forget to use gestures. In other words the speaker generally bores the audience, resulting in them not listening to their message. Since the sole purpose of giving a speech is to relay some sort of information to an audience, speaking from a manuscript should only be used in very specific situations. If you are going to be extensively quoted and it is vitally important that you be able to defend exactly what you said (think government/politics), then you are best served by a manuscript delivery. Otherwise, avoid choosing this style of delivery completely. In fact, reading your speech to your audience is rarely an appropriate choice for most speakers.

Memorized

A short jump from a manuscript delivery is memorization. Our experience in the public speaking classroom is that students often choose a *memorized delivery* when they have been told they are not allowed to read their speech to the audience. Often these novice speakers panic and decide they will memorize what they wrote. They believe they will have security using this method. Memorized speeches are rarely effective due to the unreliability of memory. We often forget what comes next and repeat the last item we remember, confusing ourselves and our audience. Delivery suffers while we frown and try to remember the next sentence. When we recite from memory, our voice adopts a cadence and we speak in a singsong rhythm which is often annoying to the audience. There are situations where memorization is appropriate, such as when acting, but usually it is a good idea to avoid this type of delivery for a speech.

Extemporaneous

Extemporaneous delivery refers to a delivery that is prepared and practiced, yet not memorized. This is the most versatile of all four delivery styles and the one that is effective in most situations. This delivery style overcomes the disadvantages of the other three styles by allowing the speaker to use notes or an outline. The speaker feels more comfortable with speaking but doesn't require memorizing the material or speaking on the spur of the moment. This results in a more "personal" delivery to the audience. The speaker is free to make eye contact and to react to audience feedback. Vocal tones and gestures seem natural and the audience feels like the speaker is having a conversation with them and not being lectured to or told what to do by the speaker. This style of delivery is the most commonly used by effective public speakers.

Once you know which type of delivery you will use, you need to think about how you will actually deliver your information. Delivery consists of two categories, verbal elements and nonverbal elements. We'll first focus on those elements of your presentation that deal with the words you will use during your delivery. The words you speak and how you say them can help you establish a rapport with your audience and help you efficiently convey your message.

Verbal Elements of Delivery

One way that we can send a message to others is through the use of *verbal elements.* This form of communication uses *language*, a written or spoken system of symbols (words), to convey a message. How we use language greatly affects the delivery of our speech.

Language

A smooth delivery depends partly on the words you use. Speakers must be aware of how they arrange words so that the audience will perceive their intended meaning. This aspect of language is called *semantics,* the meaning of words. Just because everyone in your audience may speak or understand English does not guarantee that they will understand what you are saying.

Words are symbolic. They describe the mental images that we encode in our head (see chapter 1). Your audience members will *individually* decode your spoken message and create their own mental image from your words. For example, if you say you have three dogs, your audience will envision a range of critters, from toy poodles to Saint Bernards. How can you be sure that the audience understands that you are talking about German shepherds? Even if you use the dictionary definition of a word, you cannot be sure everyone will know what you mean. Dictionaries carry several definitions for any one word. It is your duty, as a speaker, to make sure your audience understands your intended meaning. Avoid using slang and jargon in your speech and define any technical terms you may be using. Choose precise and descriptive terms, but don't choose words that are over your listeners' heads, or they won't understand what you're saying. Conversely, choosing words that your audience may feel are simplistic implies they are idiots. You don't want to have a defensive audience!

To set the mood for your topic choose your words carefully. Think about the message you are trying to deliver to your specific audience. Your previous preparation and audience analysis can help you target your information to your audience and give you insight as to what language is appropriate for the particular group to which you are speaking.

Grammar

A discussion on language would not be complete without considering grammar. *Grammar* is the system of word structure and arrangement for the language you are speaking. Standard grammar is very important. You would not walk into a room and say, "You, morning how are good?" and expect anyone to understand you. Rather, you would say, "Good morning, how are you?" Those rules and skills you learned in your English classes will pay off nicely in the realm of public speaking. Remember that speech delivery should occur as a formalized presentation, and therefore standard formal English should be used.

All languages have dialects, or words and phrases, that are commonly used and accepted by people who live in a specific geographic region. For example, the phrases "I seen" and "I come" might be used as the past tense of see and come more frequently in some sections of the United States instead of the grammatically correct "I saw" and "I came." While phrases such as these may be understandable or acceptable to some audiences, they are not grammatically correct and should not be used when delivering your speech. Using proper grammar, such as the right verb tense—past, present, or future—and speaking in complete sentences will enhance your delivery and the ultimate outcome of your speech.

Remember, most of us don't typically speak formal English on a day-to-day basis; therefore, we may need to think about what pronouns to use. For example, the proper order for the subjects of a sentence are: "My friends and

I," not "Me and my friends." Make sure your subjects and your verbs agree. Use of Standard English conveys credibility and is one way to establish your authority as a speaker. The point is to make sure your grammar doesn't hinder your speech. If the audience starts becoming annoyed with improper grammar, they aren't likely to see you as an authority to whom they should listen.

Transitions

One of your responsibilities as a speaker is to help the audience understand your ideas. You need to lead your audience as you shift from one idea to another so that they won't become lost. Shifting from one point to another is called making a *transition.* Transitions are used when you are moving to another subject, much like moving to another paragraph in your textbook. Often, beginning speakers fall into the trap of using the same transition word over and over, such as *and, but,* or *then.* In moving from one point to another, you can use other connecting phrases, many of which will enhance the relationship of the elements in your speech. We have provided you with a list of sample transitions that can be used to shift your speech from one point to another during your delivery.

Sample Transitions

on the other hand	in comparison
in addition	for example
in other words	furthermore
however	another reason
we might overlook	some think
first, second . . .	I suggest
as a result	consequently

A good way to help you break out of the *and trap* is to write more creative transition words and phrases in the margins of your note cards. Then at the podium you can quickly glance at these transition cues to help you move smoothly and meaningfully from one segment of your speech to another. Glancing at your notes is perfectly acceptable, but be careful not to glance too often, as this is distracting to your audience.

Articulation

If your audience can't understand what you are saying because you mumble or run your words together, you aren't going to keep their attention. *Articulation,* which is the process of forming clear individual sounds that are distinctly spoken words, is a skill that needs to be mastered quickly for effective delivery. There are two considerations when practicing clear articulation. First you must make sure you are saying the words correctly, which is *pronunciation,* separating and accenting the syllables in the correct manner. Once you are sure of how a word should be pronounced, the actual act of pronouncing the individual vowel and consonant sounds is called *enunciation.* If your diction is clear, your words will probably be properly enunciated. If you have an individual concern or problem in this area, your instructor can help you.

Speakers who aren't concerned about both pronunciation and enunciation make the job of paying attention as an audience member very difficult! Since your listeners ultimately decide the meaning of the words you are using, correct pronunciation keeps them on track with your line of thinking. If you are using difficult or technical words, check with an authority in this area for the correct pronunciation, or at least look the words up in the dictionary. Inevitably, if you don't, someone in your audience will be familiar with the word and realize you have made a mistake. What if you are persuading people to vote for you for student senate, and the one person who realizes that you mispronounced a word is the deciding vote? At the very least, it can be embarrassing and that only adds to speech anxiety, which is certainly something you want to avoid. Better to check before you give your speech, than to be sorry later. Following is a list of commonly mispronounced words.

Commonly Mispronounced Words

aluminum (ah-loom-in-um)	epitome (i-PIT-o-mee)
anonymous (ah-NON-uh-muss)	escape (es-KAPE)
athlete (ATH-leet)	et cetera (et-SET-er-a)
athletics (ath-LET-iks)	facade (fah-SOD)
autopsy (AW-top-see)	faux pas (FO-PAH)
banquet (BAN-kuit)	fungi (FUN-GUY)
Beethoven (BAY-toe-vin)	genuine (JEN-u-in)
blase (blah-zay)	heir (air)
brochure (bro-SHUR)	homage (OHM-aj)
cache (kash)	hysteria (hi-STARE-ee-ah)
chagrin (sha-GRIN)	impotent (IMP-o-tent)
chasm (KA-zum)	indict (in-DITE)
chef (shef)	infamous (IN-fa-muss)
chic (sheek)	Italian (it-AL-ee-in)
Chopin (SHO-pan)	lingerie (LON-jer-ay)
comparable (KOM-pra-bull)	mischievous (MISS-chi-vuss)
disastrous (diz-AA-struss)	often (OFF-en)
drama (DRAH-ma)	picture (PICK-shur)
electoral (eh-LEC-tore-all)	pitcher (PIT-chure)
elite (ee-LEET)	poignant (POYN-yant)

police (poe-LEESS)
precocious (pre-KO-shuss)
preferable (PREFF-er-a-bull)
probably (PRAH-bab-lee)
recognize (REH-cog-nize)
statistics (sta-TI-sticks)

subtle (SUH-till)
sword (sord)
theater (THEE-e-ter)
vehement (VEE-a-mint)
virile (VEER-ill)
Worcestershire (WUSS-ter-sure)

There are probably many more words that could be added to this list. However, the important issue is that if you are not sure how a word is pronounced, find out!

Fillers

We've discussed choosing our words carefully to get our message across and keep the audience listening. Now we need to take a look at words (and sounds) that we want to avoid when presenting our speech. Inexperienced speakers frequently use *fillers,* such as "um," "ah," "you know," "like," and others, that are ineffective and weaken their delivery. Time fillers make you appear hesitant and unprepared. They will annoy your audience. If they're frequent, audience members may begin counting them rather than listening to your speech. We use fillers because our minds work faster than our mouths. A simple cure for fillers is to calm down and close your mouth. If your mouth is closed while you are mentally catching up you can't "um" or "ah." "You know" and "like" are considered slang and are just as annoying as other fillers in a formal presentation. They, too, should be avoided.

It is fair to say that most speakers are totally unaware of the fillers they use. However ignorance doesn't change the fact that repetitive fillers are one of the most annoying factors heard during a speech delivery. They turn audiences off and that's certainly not your goal as a speaker. You need to become observant of your own delivery. The only way to do that is to practice your speech out loud and tune in to what you are saying. Recording yourself is an excellent way of to learn if fillers are a problem for you.

Vocals

When you are speaking aloud the sounds produced by your voice convey a message. As a speaker, you depend on your voice. The sound of your voice is produced by air that has been stored in your lungs. The capacity of the lungs is determined by a muscle located under the lungs and rib cage. This muscle is called the *diaphragm.* Like other muscles in your body, the diaphragm will tense as you become nervous. This tension causes the muscle to shrink, diminishing the potential air supply of your lungs. Air (as breath) is the primary source of the sounds we make, or our *vocals.*

To produce sounds successfully, we must know how to regulate and control this flow of air. Breathing normally requires no conscious control or awareness. It is an automatic response of our body, one that keeps us alive. However, if we add the element of speaking, we must consciously control the breathing process to produce effective, pleasing vocal tones. Air from the lungs will pass through the windpipe and into the *larynx*, which contains the membranes known as the vocal cords. As this air passes over the larynx, sounds called tones are produced. The mouth then concentrates these tones into words. The cavity of the sinuses and the head provide chambers to further refine and enhance the sound as it leaves your body, thus creating what others hear as your voice. The voice must be used effectively in order to have variety and clarity in your speech. Breathing correctly and using air to mold the sounds of your voice when speaking is an important factor in effective delivery.

The Voice

How you use your *voice* affects the verbal delivery of your speech. *Fluidity* is the ease and smoothness of the verbal delivery. While a singsong cadence isn't the most effective way to deliver a speech, neither is a choppy delivery full of unnecessary pauses. Practicing out loud will help you feel comfortable with what you are saying and help with the fluidity of your voice and speech, making it more appealing to your audience. *Tone* is important as well and consists of three elements: rate, volume, and pitch. These elements, when used together, create pleasing vocal sounds. *Rate* is the speed at which your words are actually delivered. Most people speak at a rate of approximately 200–250 words per minute. Speakers often increase the rate at which they are speaking when they become nervous or caught up in their speech. If a speaker speaks too quickly the audience can't understand him or her due to the speed of the delivery. However, effective use of rate, both speeding up and slowing down, can create interest for your audience. *Pitch* refers to the range of your voice, or where a sound you make would be placed on a musical scale. Although we don't normally think of the spoken word as musical, all sounds we create can be evaluated for relative "highness" or "lowness." This range of sound creates the pitch of your voice. While deep, low voices are often considered interesting and attractive, high-pitched sounds are considered screechy and annoying. When we become nervous or excited the pitch of our voice often rises, possibly reducing your audience's desire to listen. *Volume* refers to the softness or loudness of the tones produced when sound resonates in your sinus cavities. Although we have some control over the volume of our voice, some people have voices that are naturally loud, and others may speak louder than they need to due to physical challenges such as hearing impairment. To be an effective public speaker we need to project loudly enough to be heard by those in the last row, without blasting out those sitting in the front.

Pauses, the time in between sounds, are also a factor in vocal delivery. Placing short pauses in your speech can be an effective way to emphasize important points. However they should not be over used nor should they last for more than a few seconds. Unintentional pauses caused by a momentary lapse in memory can be a problem. Don't panic, the audience probably won't even notice if you don't fill the pause with unnecessary fillers. However, if you experience a lot of those pauses, you probably need to make a mental note to practice your speech more. Numerous pauses are received by the audience as lack of preparation. This could result in a loss of credibility and ultimately your audience.

Effective speakers will utilize all of the verbal elements to create interest for their speech. However, like any other form of communication, when mis-

---

Strengthen Your Skills

Alice in Wonderland

Purpose: The purpose of this exercise is to experience the importance of vocal inflections to create mood in delivery.

Procedure:

1. Recall the scene in *Alice in Wonderland* in which Alice meets the caterpillar. He is seated on top of a mushroom, smoking a water pipe (a remarkably contemporary pastime). Alice, now just three inches tall, peeks over the mushroom and addresses the caterpillar.

2. Try reading this selection with only a change in rate to differentiate the characters. (Read the caterpillar, because he's high, at just half the speed of Alice.)

   Caterpillar: Whoooo are yooooou?

   Alice: I'm not quite sure, Sir. You see, I was Alice when I got up this morning, but I've been changed several times since then.

   Caterpillar: What do you mean by that? Explain yourself.

   Alice: Well, I can't explain myself, because I'm not myself, you see.

   Caterpillar: I *don't* see.

   Alice: And being all these sizes in one day is confusing.

   Caterpillar: It isn't.

   Alice: It isn't what?

   Caterpillar: It isn't confusing.

   Alice: Well, perhaps your feelings make it different. All I know is it's very queer to me.

   Caterpillar: You? Whoooo are yooooou?

   —Lewis Carroll, *Alice's Adventures in Wonderland*

used they can annoy your audience. Remember, the language you use can put your audience at ease or scare them away! Preparation and practice are the stepping stones to effective verbal delivery.

Nonverbal Elements of Delivery

While there are several verbal elements that we've explored, we still need to consider another group of factors. Elements that are not specifically related to language can also enhance what you say to your audience. *Nonverbal elements* are exactly what the word implies, not verbal. Simply put, they are *not* language. In fact, elements other than words consume up to 80 percent of our day-to-day communication. These elements are significant factors in how we convey messages. Many of our nonverbal behaviors are expressed without a conscious decision to communicate. They are often interpreted by others differently than how we intend. This makes thinking about and practicing them as a part of your speech delivery important to the outcome of your speech. In addition, nonverbal communication is continuous and uses multiple channels simultaneously, which makes everything more complex.

Appearance

Your overall *appearance* can affect how your speech is accepted by your audience. First impressions are often lasting impressions. The way the members of your audience initially perceive you will affect how they respond to you. Your appearance can also affect whether they trust or respect you. Presenting the best image you can is important. Remember our discussion on audience analysis? The speaker should be aware of the usual "dress code" of the audience. Will the audience be dressed casually or formally? As the speaker, you will want to conform to the audience's standard of dress. You would not want to wear shorts and a tank top to give a speech to an audience dressed in business suits. You would probably not get past the guards at the gate! Keep this in mind on the day you are to present speeches in your classroom as well. Do not dress differently than you normally do for class, unless you are using a gimmick or using your clothes as a visual aid. Dressing up on presentation day may cause your audience to wonder why you have on a suit or dress when you normally wear jeans and a T-shirt. This will detract from, rather than aid, your delivery, unless your clothing is part of your speech. In some cases, clothing can be a dramatic element used to convey a mood to your audience. If you were speaking about the history of the 1960s, you might dress in a tie-dyed T-shirt, wear a headband, and wear a peace-sign necklace. If you are speaking about donating blood, you might wear a nurse's uniform or dress as Dracula (which one student actually did). These details can add pizzazz to your speech and help your audience get interested in what you have to say.

Avoid anything in your attire that might distract the audience from focusing on you. T-shirts with logos or graphics that don't relate to your topic, ball caps that shade your eyes, hairstyles that cover your face and cause you to flick your hair, are all things to avoid. We also recommend that you wear comfortable clothes. The day you deliver your speech is not the day you want to wear new shoes. You are trying to concentrate on what you are saying and do not need any uncomfortable distractions.

Facial Expressions

Your face is a valuable asset to your delivery. Your *facial expressions,* or the animation of your features, allow you to convey emotion without the use of any words. We let our faces tell a story just as much as our lan-

This speaker has added sunglasses to his appearance because his speech topic is Hitchhiking in Southern California. Are the sunglasses an effective visual aid or a distraction?

guage does. However, when you approach the podium to give your speech, you do not want to show you are nervous by wearing an expressionless stone mask. This physical reaction to fear will severely limit your ability to tell your story. Your audience will be watching your facial expressions. If you can show you are interested in your topic through your facial expressions, your audience will become interested as well. Animated use of the face will cue your audience that you are sincere and will serve as an invitation for them to join in your message, thus also helping you to relax.

Eye Contact

Many of you probably have heard the expression that the eyes are the windows to the soul. The eyes truly are the most important aspect of the face, and making *eye contact* with another person—looking directly at him or her—conveys a wealth of emotion and communication to that person—a sense of sincerity that does not occur when looking at the wall, at notes, or over the heads of listeners. Looking at all members in the audience individually at some point during your speech is wise, even if this means you are able to look at each one only briefly. You can shift your gaze from one member to another throughout your entire speech. For a few moments, each audience member will feel like you are speaking directly to him or her. Do not look at your listener's forehead, do not look at his or her arm; look directly into his or her eyes. Look at all eyes in the room. Looking at people invites, almost commands, them to look back at you and pay attention. When they look and pay attention, they are listening, and this gives you valuable feedback. Feedback is essential to getting your point across to your audience. The best procedure is to maintain frequent eye contact with as many members of your audience as possible, thereby keeping their interest and receiving their responses.

Posture

The manner in which you hold your body is known as *posture.* Good posture, (remember when your mother told you to stand up straight and not slouch?) is very useful in public speaking. Most likely, your instructor will ask you to use a podium or lectern when you speak. It will be important to place your notes on this device and stand directly behind it, straight and tall. Do not lean on or over the podium. Leaning over the podium suggests sloppiness and insincerity to your audience, and leaning on the podium could cause you to push it directly off of its stand! On the other hand, you don't want to hold yourself in a stiff or rigid position either. Standing up straight and tall should look natural, not forced. To take a comfortable stance, place your feet directly below your shoulders and distribute your weight evenly. By doing this you will avoid any unnecessary movements that often accompany nervousness, such as shifting your weight from foot to foot, or swaying side to side or back and forth.

Gestures

The movements of the hand(s) or body to add emphasis to important points are known as *gestures.* Most of us use our hands a great deal in informal speaking, but this is one of the least used tactics by beginning speakers. If we are trying to give directions to a friend, we often point and raise our arms to indicate the direction in which we want our friend to turn. When some speakers get up to the podium, they grip the sides of it until their knuckles turn white, clasp their hands behind their back, jangle the change in their pocket, or drum their fingers on the podium. In doing this, they ignore the valu-

This gesture might accentuate a particular point or be a nonverbal means of asking the audience, "What do *you* think?"

able everyday habit of using gestures to emphasize or complement what they are saying.

Movement attracts attention, and gestures can be used in a positive way to get that attention when you need it the most. Let's say you are trying to convey to your audience the importance of study skills in college. As you say the words "this is important," you can make a fist with your hand and wave it in the air. Your audience is attracted to this movement and subconsciously associates the strength and force of your fist with the word *important*. You achieve your desired result with a well-placed gesture. There are hundreds of gestures available to you as a speaker, but be careful not to overuse them. Remember that gestures can be used to add emphasis, but you certainly don't want every word or sentence in your speech emphasized. Furthermore, you want to be sure that no gestures you use convey obscene or inappropriate meanings to your audience.

You can also gesture with your body. A quick step back from the podium might emphasize a message of caution or alarm. However, although gesturing is important, too much movement can distract audience members. They will pay attention to your movements and not to what you are saying. Moving away from the podium can cause you to lose the interest of your audience as well, and should only be done for emphasis, unless you are giving a lecture. Notes should always remain on the podium and not be carried or held. Moving toward your audience implies informality and is not the normal posture for public speaking. Use your movements appropriately. Don't be stiff but don't move so frequently that your audience suffers motion sickness from watching you.

Strengthen Your Skills

Tell Them Where You Parked

Purpose: The purpose of this exercise is to show you the importance and natural use of gestures by trying to avoid their use.

Procedure:

1. Stand behind the podium and clasp your hands behind your back.

2. Using *no* hand gestures, give directions from where you are standing to your parked car.

3. Does this seem awkward and strange? It should, because gestures are very commonly used by all of us.

Answering Questions from the Audience

Now that we know which nonverbal elements we can incorporate into our delivery, the final item we must deal with occurs after the delivery is over—questions! It is important to prepare for questions from your audience.

While your public speaking class may not include time for questions from your audience after your speech, a question-and-answer period is often a standard feature of many speaking engagements. In order to help you prepare for these situations, we'll offer some suggestions for making them go as smoothly as possible.

1. **Be prepared, which means really know your topic.** That's one of the reasons you need to know a speech topic better than an essay topic. Think about the type of questions you might be asked and prepare a response to them.

2. **After hearing the question, repeat it to make sure everyone in the audience knows what you are responding to before you give your answer.**

3. **Give straightforward, concise answers.** This is a question-and-answer period, not a discussion. Allow only one follow-up question per person (if requested) and move on. You want to answer as many questions as you can in the time allowed.

4. **If you don't understand the question, say, "I'm not sure I understand what you are asking. Here's what I think the question is [fill in with your perception]. Is that correct?"** If you don't know the answer, say so, don't try and fake it.

5. **Even if you perceive a question as hostile in some way, don't react to it that way.** Never use sarcasm or any other tone that may be interpreted by your audience as a negative response. You are the speaker and you can control the situation by not allowing yourself to be manipulated.

Conclusion

We have discussed numerous elements that are very important for your speech to be effective, but it is the verbal and nonverbal elements of your delivery that ultimately convey your message to your audience. Everything you do at the podium sends a message. Paying attention to these elements when you practice your speech will result in a speech that is more effective when you actually deliver it and will engage the audience and convey your message.

Application to Everyday Life

Students frequently bring a sheet of paper to class that contains a series of hatch marks (IIII) covering the entire page. These marks represent every time an instructor has said "um" or "uh" during a lecture. When poor speaking skills get in the way of the message, the speaker (instructor) and the audience (students) lose. The next time you are in a situation that requires you to listen for important information, don't let an ineffective delivery keep you from listening. Obviously this isn't easy to do, but you are only harming yourself when you fail to comprehend the message by tuning out.

DISCUSSION QUESTIONS

1. Discuss how rate, volume, and pitch combine to create the tone of your voice.
2. Why are the verbal and nonverbal elements of delivery as important as the content of your speech?
3. As an audience member, what are some vocal elements that, when used by a speaker, make it difficult to stay interested in what he or she is saying?
4. As an audience member, what are some nonverbal elements that distract you or interfere with you listening to a speaker?
5. Why is it important to practice your speech out loud?

KEY WORDS

- appearance
- articulation
- delivery
- diaphragm
- enunciation
- extemporaneous delivery
- eye contact
- facial expressions
- fillers
- fluidity
- gestures
- grammar
- impromptu speech
- language
- larynx
- manuscript delivery
- memorized delivery
- nonverbal elements
- pauses
- pitch
- posture
- pronunciation
- rate
- semantics
- tone
- transitions
- verbal elements
- vocals
- voice
- volume

12

The More the Merrier?

Group Speeches

- Some of your future speaking will involve speaking as a member of a group.
- Small group communication occurs frequently in modern-day society.
- Small group communication is an area in which most people lack skill.
- A small group consists of three to fifteen people who meet together for whatever time is necessary to accomplish some shared specific task or goal.
- Three elements that contribute to the success or failure of a group are group composition, group size, and group time restraints.
- Groups are usually created for one of three reasons: to accomplish a specific task, to handle a crisis situation, or to manage or resolve conflict.
- There are four methods that groups can use to make decisions.
- The leadership role is not always assigned, yet a leader will emerge.
- Task roles are roles that emerge to help the group organize its work and accomplish its goals.
- Maintenance roles allow the group to interact in a smooth and supportive manner.
- Personal roles bring frustration when individuals disregard the larger goal of the group.

The conference is running along smoothly. Currently, Barry Foster is speaking about the company's direct deposit program. He has asked John and Pam to organize each division's employees into small groups according to the departments they work in. He has assigned each group a leader and wants that person to help the others fill out a questionnaire and some sign-up forms. Hopefully all of this can be accomplished in the time frame he has been allotted. John is concerned that there won't be enough time to finish the project. Pam is concerned that each of the leaders of the groups won't be able to keep control of the group members. She remembers participating in groups in the past where everything has gone completely wrong! Will this be the same kind of mess?

As we begin the final chapter of the text, we hope you've learned some valuable new skills as we followed John and Pam while they planned the conference. The skills we have learned can be used for all your communication, not just public speaking. One additional skill that will be useful to you is the ability to work in a group in addition to speaking to one. This will be the focus of our final chapter.

Why Study Small Group Communication?

Throughout this study of public speaking, we have prepared you for speaking as an individual to a collective group of people, your audience. However, some of your future speaking will involve working collectively with others as a member of a group. This process is known as *small group communication* and it occurs frequently in modern-day society. It is estimated that twenty million meetings occur every day. These meetings occur in hundreds of locations, for just as many reasons, throughout the world. The advent of software that allows synchronous communication via the Internet has made global communication, without travel, possible. Research shows that executives may spend two-thirds of their day in some type of meeting. These meetings occur because people come together to solve a problem, discuss an issue, or plan an event. These people work toward a common goal, not individual gratification. Reaching this common goal is the primary function of the group.

While we tend to think of groups as formal entities associated with work, school, or organizations, we all belong to "informal" groups. We are continually involved in small group communication with our family and friends. These groups are just one reason why we need to understand how groups function as a part of our lives.

Business and industry frequently require small groups to run their companies. Their employees are expected to function effectively within these groups. Effective small group collaboration skills are mentioned by CEOs as the skill recent college graduates lack most. If you want to be hired or promoted, the likelihood is that your own small group communication skills will be a major factor in those decisions.

Since it is most likely that you already participate in small groups and will need to continue such activity throughout your life, it seems sensible that you learn how to be effective in one. Let's look more closely at small group communication.

What Is Small Group Communication?

A small group consists of three to fifteen people who meet together for whatever time is necessary to accomplish some shared specific task or goal. While traditionally these meetings occur face to face; chat rooms, Internet bulletin boards, Listservs, and conferencing software also provide opportunities for groups to function effectively online. All such groups share similar characteristics no matter what environment they meet in or what their stated task or goal.

Why Group Work?

Although our society was founded on beliefs that the interests of individuals should take precedence over those of the state (a doctrine of *individualism*) it does utilize *collectivism* throughout its structure. When individuals live in a group, whether it be a family, a local community, or a country, the needs of the group as a whole will in some instances supersede those of each individual. Thus, our society is a blend of collectivism and individualism. Most religious and educational institutions, corporations, and governmental agencies use some form of collective group structure to accomplish their work. Although groups are formed for various reasons and to accomplish different tasks, the process for success is the same. As a reasoning member of a society that uses group process, you should be aware of how an effective group functions and be able to work within one.

Individuals in groups share information and make choices. The public nature of group work tends to make people more dedicated to the outcome of the group, and being a group member generally increases your commitment to the decisions made by the group.

Most groups form to accomplish a particular task, such as developing new procedures for fire drills, voting on whether to purchase new computers, or planning a conference. Other groups meet for the purpose of social interaction and enrichment. Examples of these types of groups include Bible study groups, business groups, book clubs, and investment clubs.

What Makes a Group Function?

There are three elements that contribute to the success or failure of any group in accomplishing its goal. These elements include group composition, group size, and group time restraints. Let's explore each of these elements more fully.

1. **Group composition**
   - All group members must act cohesively and work toward a common goal.
   - All group members must seek and share information.
   - All group members must be flexible and forgo individual decisions in favor of ideas adopted by the group.
   - All group members must share responsibility and support the group.

2. Group size

- A small group must include at least three people.
- Groups of five or seven appear to function the best.
- Odd-numbered groups are more efficient than even-numbered groups.
- In larger groups, the quieter members tend not to share their opinions.
- Groups larger than fifteen break into subgroups or cliques.

3. Group time restraints

- The length of time a group meets together will vary.
- Meeting time depends on the group's purpose and type.
- *Primary groups* such as family and friends exist for the long term.
- *Secondary groups* are formed to accomplish a specific task and exist for shorter periods of time.
- There is no minimum or maximum time frame for a group to be effective.
- A group will continue to exist until it decides its task is complete.

Being aware of these elements can help you when forming or working in a group. If a group's characteristics differ from the "ideal" group size and composition, you can keep in mind that problems can occur. For example, let's say you are part of a group consisting of nine people. Your task is to develop rules for future company meetings. Groups with larger numbers (bulleted above) may result in the quieter group members feeling intimidated. This can cause them to refuse to share their opinions. Realizing that group size may have contributed to this problem can help you to draw out the shy members of the group and encourage them to contribute their thoughts and feelings. The fact that these people aren't sharing their opinions could result in the group losing valuable input. In addition, it could cause members to withdraw from the group. Group size is just one element that contributes to the success or failure of any group.

Advantages of Small Groups

There are many advantages to working in groups. On the whole, people usually enjoy the interaction that occurs when working with other people. Human beings are for the most part very social creatures. According to most psychological studies, social interaction is one of the basic components of human need. Participating in a group gives us a chance to make our views known and share them with others. This form of interaction increases our motivation to achieve a positive outcome for the task at hand and provides us with a rewarding experience. It makes us feel good to be a functioning member of a successful group. That is why working with others in a group is usually more socially rewarding than working alone.

People enjoy the interaction that occurs when working in a small group.

In order for all group members to get along, it is often necessary to be cognizant of others and place our own needs and desires on hold. In a group, the concept of *synergy* applies—the combination of the parts working together has more value than each individual part working alone. You might think of synergy as $1 + 1 = 3$! When people come together and share their experiences and knowledge, wonderful things can and do happen. Individuals working alone often make biased judgments and decisions that can lead to inappropriate actions. In a group, the influence of the other group members can help individuals maintain an open mind and stay focused on the larger issue.

When group members get together for a common goal, many things are taking place, some at the same time, some at varying times, some by individual members, and some by the group as a whole. As these occur, different members will play different roles, just as the parts of a motor work separately but cohesively so that the motor can run efficiently. In order to examine the group further, remember that there are advantages to working in a group:

- A large amount of information can be collected.
- Many recommendations can be evaluated at once.
- An accurate and effective solution to a task can be chosen.
- Collaboration can be socially rewarding to group members.

One of the factors in reaching a decision is the quality and quantity of information collected. Five people can remember or store five times the amount of knowledge that one can. Group members may trigger or cue new information from one another, thus leading to more information being shared.

Group decisions are usually more accurate than individual decisions. You have probably heard the saying, "two heads are better than one"; that's exactly what this means. When people form a group, they contribute their opinions and ideas. They can collectively examine an issue in depth and come to a decision more effectively than one person alone can.

Whether you call it cooperation or *cohesiveness,* group members must stick together and work for the common good of the group. This means that at some point, the group must choose a course of action appropriate for the overall task at hand. Effective groups consist of people who work *together* to solve a problem, with members sharing equally in the responsibilities of the group. All members must share the chores! This cooperation fosters empathy and shared understanding, which in turn leads to better communication, increased productivity, higher morale, and group loyalty. This feeling of oneness with the group is probably the single most important factor in effective group interaction.

As group members, we are forced to think within a collective unit, setting collaborative goals and reaching common solutions to shared problems. We are forced to get along with others within the group or risk disharmony. If disharmony occurs within the group, the result can be failure to achieve the group's goal.

Disadvantages of Small Groups

There are also some disadvantages to group work of which we should be aware. The major disadvantage of group work is the time investment. Working in a group can take more time than working on your own. One person usually can arrive at a decision in less time than it takes a group. This characteristic can easily be confirmed the next time you and your friends are trying to decide where to eat dinner or what movie to see! In a group, not only must each person come to an individual decision, all members must then share their decisions and collectively reach a final decision. Individuals may be motivated by others' behaviors, their environment, or their own physical or mental state. All individual motives and factors must be addressed during the group process, and this takes more time. In addition, difficulties exist and complications can arise as people with different personalities try to arrive at mutually satisfactory conclusions.

Perhaps the most apparent difficulty to working in a group is that within any group there are often one or two group members who are freeloaders. A *freeloader* is any group member who does not participate in the group process. Freeloaders do not make individual contributions, and their lack of collaboration is frustrating. Freeloaders typically do very little, if anything, to assist the group in achieving its goal but expect to reap the benefits of the group's collec-

This woman is having a negative group experience. Because she has put her own needs and desires above those of the group, she is unable to function as a member of the group.

tive rewards. Let's consider the class member who is assigned to a group project but fails to attend group meetings. The person rarely contributes any work to the group, but expects to receive the same grade the other members receive. What about the colleague at work who avoids working on a project but expects to receive the same recognition from the boss as those who actually collaborated and got the job done? Those are both examples of freeloaders. We suspect you have your own personal examples from previous group experiences. While the lack of input from the slacking group member may diminish the amount of information and ideas a group will gather, most groups can effectively collaborate and achieve their goals without the member being active. It is not the presence of a freeloader in a group that becomes the problem. It is the resentment of the active members who, when all is said and done, believe it is unfair for someone to get credit for something he or she didn't do. It isn't fair. We agree, but we also know that the group must address the issue of freeloading if it exists and come to a consensus on what to do. Otherwise it will become a significant disadvantage to the effectiveness of your collaborative effort.

The cousin of the freeloader is the *do-it-aller.* The do-it-aller is the person who takes control of the group and insists that everything be done his or her way. These people immediately make assignments to the rest of the group and typically write the report, or prepare the presentation, using their own ideas and research. They are not in real collaboration with the rest of the group. While this behavior is often considered to be that of a poor leader, this is not the case. What is really happening in such an environment is that the group is actually leaderless. It is as if the bully has taken over the playground because there is no playground monitor present. Therefore, another disadvantage to group work is that if no leader emerges to coordinate the group process, a bully can cause the group experience to be stressful, a waste of time, and unrewarding. Any time an individual puts his or her own needs or desires above the group's, trouble forms.

Those who have had negative group experiences (and most people have) often avoid collaborative tasks, or approach them with a negative attitude, which can in and of itself cause a group to flounder. Each group task should be approached as a new experience, as a possible opportunity for success.

Types of Groups

Groups are usually created for one of three reasons: to accomplish a specific task, to handle a crisis situation, or to manage or resolve conflict.

1. **Specific task.** All members of the group collectively pursue the same goal or *specific task*. Most committee work involves a *singular motive*. *Committees* are formed in order to accomplish a specific purpose for a determined length of time. The word *committee* is often preceded with a term that indicates the committee's singular purpose, such as awards banquet committee, dance committee, or textbook adoption committee. Each of these committees meets until a predetermined deadline occurs, and the group is motivated to complete the task.

2. **Crisis situation**. Group members gather to respond to a problem that needs immediate attention, often without advance warning. Generally they have some background knowledge or individual expertise related to the topic or task that requires a meeting. In a *crisis situation,* group members are required to assess a situation and make decisions based on limited information. Once the initial crisis is under control, problem-solving groups are formed to find a more long-term solution that can be implemented to remedy the identified problem. Citizen utility boards, fund-raising groups, and neighborhood watch groups are examples of problem-solving groups formed from crisis situations. Crisis situation groups have replaced the quality control circles of the past in corporate America. These groups form to monitor quality of products, employee incentive programs, and plant safety. The real issue in a crisis situation, or problem-solving group, is that there is a perceived problem that requires a solution. Group members are then brought together to share their knowledge and expertise in order to reach a viable solution that works for all parties involved.

3. **Conflict management or resolution.** Corporations are common environments for *conflict management* groups. Individuals or representatives

of groups with conflicting interests or perspectives meet collectively to come up with strategies and techniques to manage the conflict so it doesn't escalate, or they resolve the conflict altogether, known as *conflict resolution*. Skills in bargaining and negotiating are important when trying to resolve clashing interests, needs, and goals.

We find that most groups fall in one of the categories listed above, and it is likely that most of us will need to function effectively within one or more of them during our school or business careers. Research shows that corporations rate employee skills in communication and group process much higher than possession of a master's degree in business! These corporations believe that decisions reached in groups are more effective, and therefore more valuable, than those reached by individuals. Group work also abounds in civic, religious, and educational environments. Even family groups and groups of friends function more harmoniously when they interact well with one another. You will be part of many groups in your lifetime, so you need to understand group process. Let's take a moment to explore in more detail what happens in a group.

Group Process

So how can group members arrive at decisions with a feeling of oneness? Let's examine four decision-making processes that can help accomplish collaboration within a group.

Decision-Making Processes

The first thing the group must do is understand the problem to be solved (in much the same way an individual speaker must understand the task to be accomplished or the topic of his or her speech). Because solutions to a problem, or the way to complete a task will not necessarily be evident, the group must discuss, evaluate, and weigh options to make the best decision. There are four methods the group can use to come to a decision.

1. **Majority rule.** This process requires the group to come to a decision by voting. If 51 percent or more of the total number of voters favor one issue or idea, then the *majority rules.* If there are diverse opinions or loyalties in a group, these conflicts can be solved by using this method.

2. **Consensus.** This method occurs when all members of the group unanimously agree on an issue. A *consensus* is usually arrived at through a series of discussions. No vote is necessary as everyone eventually holds the same thought or idea. Decisions arrived at through the method of consensus are usually the most effective. However, consensus is very time-consuming, even when opinions don't differ greatly.

3. **Popular vote.** This method is similar to majority rule. The major difference in a *popular vote* is that the issue adopted by the group is the one

that receives the most "popular" votes. For example, if there are twelve members in a group and four vote for idea number 1, five vote for idea number 2, and the remaining three members vote for idea number 3, then idea number 2 wins by "popular" vote. In other words, the most members voted for this issue. In fact, in this particular example, only 42 percent of the vote won the decision. This is how popular vote differs from majority rule. For majority rule, 51 percent or more of the members must vote for a singular idea. If time is running out and discussions have failed to solve an issue, a popular vote may be required.

4. **Compromise.** If none of the other methods work, members can reach a decision through *compromise*. In this method some members forego their opinions in favor of what works for the group as a whole. While this method of decision making is perhaps the most commonly used, it should be noted that it may not be the *best* choice. Decisions that aren't supported by all group members may result in less productivity and may keep the group from achieving the group's goals.

Avoiding Problems in a Group

In order to avoid problems in a group, members must be able to gather and share information. This is the only way that valid decisions can be made no matter what decision-making method is used. The process of gathering information is best handled by group members individually researching and gathering information related to a specific part of the task. There is no need to duplicate efforts, so dividing up the research is a time-saving practice. However, all information gathered will need to be shared with the group as a whole so decisions can be made in a collaborative manner. Here are some guidelines you can use when gathering and sharing information for a group meeting.

1. Get the facts before making a decision.
2. Investigate several sources of information.
3. Take notes, photocopy, or create a computer file of pertinent information.
4. Share your data with the group.

Researching and preparing individually for your group meetings will make them more productive. E-mail can be a great help in disbursing information quickly to group members prior to an actual meeting. That way meeting time can be spent working rather than reading. If group members fail to research, or if only a few members do research, the session is apt to be a waste of time or will resemble a lecture period rather than a group work session.

Group Roles

A significant part of group process involves the individual roles members will adopt within the group. The primary role that we usually think about when discussing small groups is the role of leader. However, there are many other roles you need to understand as well. These include task roles, maintenance roles, and personal roles. Understanding these roles can help you to make your group more efficient and cohesive. Let's begin with the leadership role.

Leadership Roles

The first question that comes to mind in a group is, "Who's in charge?" If the group is organized for a goal other than mere social interaction, who will get things focused and going? Although your professor or boss may not have assigned a group *leader,* one will nevertheless emerge. In a group, several personality types will be present, and one will usually dominate. This person will become the driving force for the group, or the leader. In fact, even when a leader is assigned, the real leader of the group may not be the person who actually has the label. It could be someone else!

What is this person like? What are the attributes of a good leader? First, he or she should be confident, open-minded, generous of spirit, and courteous. These sound like characteristics of a paragon—an impossibly perfect person. However, you'd be surprised how many people meet these criteria, at least in the context of a group environment.

The leader should be able to draw out other members of the group to learn what their opinions are on an issue. A person who is afraid of voicing his or her opinion and facing the opinions of others will not function well as a group leader. An effective leader facilitates tasks of the group; he or she does not assume responsibility for doing or achieving everything. Such a leader inspires trust by listening to all group members in an attempt to understand their ideas and opinions. Leaders plan, assess, motivate, and set goals in collaboration with other group members. An effective leader is one that others will follow because they want to, not because they believe they have to.

If the leader of the group is not functioning properly, what can be done? Change leaders! Your group is a democratic organization and, as such, is governed by the same rules. You have learned four ways to make a decision in a group. Use one of these decision-making processes to replace your leader. When enough of the group members feel that a change at the top is in order, that change should take place. Remember, we are functioning as a group, not as individuals, and the group's goal is more important than any one individual's search for self-gratification. With the proper leadership, your group stands a good chance of reaching the goal you set with a minimum of hassles.

While typically a leader will emerge (whether one is appointed or not) it is possible that a group may be leaderless. Although this does not often occur, if it does, it is usually the result of one of the following factors:

- Two or more group members are competing for the role of leader and the group splits in loyalty. This can make the group environment tense and ineffective.

- All members of the group assume responsibility and take turns filling the leadership role. This can facilitate group process and still result in the group accomplishing its goal.

Just as the leader has a role to play, so do the other members of the group. We are sure you will be able to recognize your friends, and perhaps yourself, in these various small group roles.

Task Roles

Those roles that emerge due to the task-oriented nature of the group are *task roles.* These roles help group members organize the work of the group to accomplish its goal. There are many task roles that are directly linked to a specific job. The following is a list of some of the most common task roles and their function/definition:

1. The *secretary* is the person who keeps track of the group's progress by recording any information pertinent to the group's outcome. This might include taking notes, recording facts and figures, or keeping track of members who are present or absent.

2. The *opinionator* expresses his or her opinions and beliefs freely and without hesitation.

3. The *initiator* gets the ball rolling by proposing new ideas or different procedures.

4. The *clarifier* makes sure other group members understand problems and ideas by verbalizing the information in a new fashion to make it clear.

5. The *informer* is loaded with a wealth of information, providing facts and statistics relevant to the group's task. (This person always wins at "Are You Smarter than a 5th Grader?")

6. The *coordinator* arranges details such as seating, room arrangement, and equipment necessary to complete the task. This person may make copies, overhead transparencies, and so on.

7. The *energizer* is just like the bunny! This person keeps going and going and going, and makes the other group members go with him or her.

8. The *inquirer* is not a tabloid publication, but a person who makes requests for short but detailed information by asking questions, seeking opinions, and looking for facts. This person keeps the group singularly focused.

9. The *evaluator* reminds the group of standards they have set and measures suggestions against such standards.

10. The *tracker* shifts the group's discussions and attention back to the task when things have gone off track.

In groups where task roles are shared equitably, satisfaction with the group process is high. There is increased cohesion among members and a successful group outcome is the usual result.

Maintenance Roles

Group cohesion develops in such a way that *maintenance roles* evolve; these roles are necessary for the overall good of the group and allow the group to interact in a smooth and supportive way. Maintenance roles keep the group working harmoniously. Where task roles are necessary to achieve a desired outcome or goal, maintenance roles are necessary to create an environment in which group members can be happy and productive while working. The following is a list of some maintenance roles assumed by members of the group:

1. The *stress buster* functions much like a medieval court jester. Just as the jester kept the king happy and in a good mood, this person uses humor to keep the group in a good mood.

2. The *harmonizer* does not sing; rather, this person helps group members settle conflicts and acts as an overall mediator.

3. The *gatekeeper* controls the flow of communication, often opening the door for members to contribute new ideas. Sometimes, this function requires closing the door. This person may ask members to share ideas, while at the same time keep others from dominating discussions. Controlling both elements is necessary for the group to function smoothly.

4. The *cheerleader* does just that—encourages other members to contribute and lets them know their ideas are valuable and appreciated.

5. The *collaborator* is one who points out similarities in group members' ideas in order to make mutually agreeable decisions and solutions.

6. The *parent* is friendly and shows care and concern for group members. This person will ask a group member about how something went, or ask how members are feeling each time the group meets. This is the member who often provides refreshments!

Assumption of maintenance roles is as essential to effective group process as the leadership role and task roles. They are the "heart" of the group process. They keep the group functioning by provide encouragement to the individuals who make up the group.

Personal Roles

Unfortunately, since groups are composed of human beings, *personal roles* will also emerge based on individual personalities. Personal roles generally bring frustration to group work. The selfish characteristics of some people, and their disregard for the larger good of the group, can cause chaos for the other group members. These saboteurs can seriously impair productivity and even be responsible for the group not meeting its goals. The following is a list of personal, self-centered roles and the *dysfunction* that they cause:

1. The *monopolizer* is the person who consumes the group by taking too much time by assuming a role that is not suited to his or her skills.

2. The *joker*, unlike the stress buster (who uses humor to put other group members at ease), uses humor inappropriately to get laughs and distract members from their work.

3. The *loafer* refuses to contribute or participate (also known as a freeloader).

4. The *antagonizer* is the thorn in everyone's side and promotes arguments and conflict with all group members.

5. The *roadblock* has strong personal opinions and views and is unwilling to abandon these views for the good of the group. This creates an impasse that is difficult to maneuver around, much like the *do not cross* signs at a real roadblock!

6. The *self-seeker* always wants the attention of the group on him or her. This person may brag about past accomplishments or tell personal stories unrelated to the task at hand simply to keep members focused and listening to him or her. It's all about meeeeeeeee!

7. The *poor me*, like the self-seeker, shifts attention to him- or herself. However, the purpose in doing so is to get members' sympathy. Poor me's are the people who always have an excuse as to why they can't meet with the group or haven't been able to do what they were asked to do at the last meeting. They may use illness, working two jobs, being a single parent, or school work to justify their lack of participation in the group. This role can easily eat up group collaboration time because the group "parent" spends valuable group meeting time attempting to lift the poor me out of his or her rut.

Now that we have investigated leadership roles, task roles, maintenance roles, and personal roles, our discussion of small group communication is nearly done. After reading about the benefits, problems, and roles present in group process, you may have come to the conclusion that working in a group is too complicated and stressful. You may be thinking that it's easier to work as an individual and avoid all group situations. All decisions, whether made individually or in a group, pose certain risks and benefits. But unless you are planning to become a hermit in the mountains of Colorado or on the craggy shores of New England, at some point you will need to function in a group situation. Also, whether you are aware of it or not, all of the factors that we have examined are already at work in the groups that you currently belong to. Knowing the concepts at work within group process can help you to work more effectively in any group, for whatever reason, to meet the goals that have been established.

Strengthen Your Skills

Problem Solving in a Group

Purpose: It is inevitable that you will have to collaborate in many groups during your life. Knowing what works will help these situations be much more enjoyable. This exercise will allow you to participate in a group project and observe group process, learning what helps and what hinders group work.

Procedure:

You work for an advertising agency and your boss wants you to find a successful way to help your clients sell products to their own customers. He wants you and your team to find out the best persuasive techniques used to sell products. He's a little dense (please don't tell him I said that) so he will also require examples demonstrating each technique you recommend. He's sent you a memo about the project.

From: The Boss@headquarters.com Sent: 6–03–08 8:00 am

To: valuedemployee@spch131.edu

cc: othervaluedemployees

Subject: Very Important Project

As you are aware, our bottom line is slipping lower and lower. Our clients are not renewing their contracts. If we don't find a way to be more persuasive in our clients' advertising campaigns, we will have to begin lay-offs. Therefore, I've divided the office into two teams, the "couch surfers" and the "Web surfers." It is your job to find the persuasive techniques that are effective for each situation. So get started! Time is money!

Your instructor will divide you into groups. Some groups will be the "couch surfers" (searching for TV ads) and others will be the "Web surfers" (searching for Internet ads). In your report:

1. List at least five (5) techniques used in persuasion.

2. Define each of the techniques in detail.

3. Write a description, in detail, of three advertisements your group found (Web surfers from Web ads, couch surfers from TV ads). The ads chosen must, between them, use the 5 techniques you identified. Web surfers provide the URL for your sites. Couch surfers describe where you saw the two commercials.

4. Explain why and how your ads use the persuasive techniques you identified.

5. Summarize what your group learned about persuasion from this exercise.

6. Conclude your report with recommendations to your boss on how to use the information you have provided to maintain and increase the agency's client base.

Guidelines for Effective Groups

While every group will be unique, they all work (or don't work) for the same reasons. Once you are engaged in a group, the following checklist can be most effective and result in successful group collaboration.

1. **Get off to a good start.**

    • Exchange names, e-mail addresses, phone numbers (cell and land-line), and any other contact information members will need.

    • Immediately discuss and establish the group's task/goals. Don't just assume that everyone has the same understanding of what the group's outcomes should be. Establish expectations in the first group meeting.

2. **Make it manageable.**

    • Divide the task into several small parts.

    • Create a timeline for when each part must be completed.

    • Agree on what each member will be responsible for.

    • Decide what the procedure will be if a member does not accomplish his or her individual group work in a timely manner.

    • Set up dates and times for regular group meetings. While some work will be accomplished individually, all members must be aware of and collaborate on the final report, project, or presentation. People are busy; let them know what they are adding to their schedule.

3. **Pay attention to the process.**

    • Identify a leader and engage in task and maintenance roles to facilitate the group's mission.

    • Avoid personal roles, but if they evolve, point them out and deal with them.

    • At each group meeting assess what has been accomplished so far. This limits procrastination and allows for changes if necessary.

    • Look for "missing parts." In your review sessions pay attention to things that may have fallen through the cracks and weren't originally considered. The earlier these omissions are addressed the better.

    • Modify original appointments and timelines as necessary, so completing the task won't result in rushing to complete it the night before it is due.

Effective collaboration can be rewarding. Groups often find the best solutions to problems. However being an effective group member requires time and dedication to the group's goals. As Henry Ford said about teamwork, "Coming together is a beginning. Keeping together is progress. Working together is success."

Conclusion

A working knowledge of group process as presented in this chapter will help everyone be a more effective group member. This should result in successful group collaboration and a rewarding experience for all. We've tried to provide you with information that will make you a successful group member and make your day-to-day communication effective and satisfying. Remember that the goal of all communication is understanding. This is true whether you are speaking in a formal presentation to a large audience, speaking with one person, or functioning as a member of a group.

Application to Everyday Life

We suspect that as you read about the roles that occur in groups, you were able to remember when you or others took on such roles. Some of those leadership, task, and maintenance roles helped you and others resolve conflict or achieve a goal by finding a solution to a problem. At other times personal roles may have interfered. However, we often forget that our own interactions with family and friends work or don't work for the same reasons that we've presented for formal group work. Think about a problem you've experienced when trying to resolve an issue with friends and/or family. How can applying what you've learned about effective small group communication make such interactions more successful in the future?

DISCUSSION QUESTIONS

1. Name three groups of which you are a member and the roles you perform in each.
2. Name two task roles and their function. How do they help a group achieve its goal?
3. Name two maintenance roles and their function. How do they help a group achieve its goals?
4. Why are personal roles dysfunctional for the group as a whole?
5. Discuss the benefits of working in a group.

KEY WORDS

- cohesiveness
- collectivism
- committees
- compromise
- conflict management
- conflict resolution
- consensus
- crisis situation
- do-it-aller
- freeloader
- individualism
- leader
- maintenance roles
- majority rule
- personal roles
- popular vote
- primary groups
- secondary groups
- singular motive
- small group communication
- specific task
- synergy
- task roles

Epilogue

The Rest of the Story . . .

They did it! It's over! The conference was a tremendous success. John and Pam have been given a standing ovation, and the vice president has given them three days off and a bonus for all of their hard work.

Pam is going out of town. She's hitting the Mega Mall and spending her bonus. She is going to buy her fiancé a nice gift as well, since she has not been able to spend much time with him lately. John is going fishing to relax. He has earned it! He can't wait to see his wife's eyes light up when he shows her his bonus check. Now they can buy that new surround-sound theater system for the family room. The kids will love it!

Both Pam and John are lost in their thoughts. The vice president has made some kind of announcement and has called for a majority vote. Oh no, they should have been paying attention. They have just been voted as co-chairs for next year's conference! Here we go again!

Postscript from the Authors

Our goals, after we completed our audience analysis for the revision of this text, were to provide you with straightforward information to help you communicate more effectively. That includes formal public speaking (the main focus of the text), small group communication, and day-to-day interpersonal communication. We know from research and experiences that effective communication skills are learned in a public speaking class. These are skills that we want you to use whenever clear and effective communication is necessary. We believe our journey together was successful. However, without feedback from you, our audience, we won't know what worked and what didn't. To that end, we invite comments, suggestions, and questions from you. Please e-mail *tsmith@lc.edu* with your feedback.

Appendix A
Class Assignments

Critique Assignment

1. You are to critique (evaluate) one other student's speech.

2. You may critique someone's informative or persuasive speech.

3. The critique should be written in essay form and include comments about the content and delivery of the speech. Support your comments with examples as necessary.

4. Your instructor will be the only one who will see your critique. It will not be seen by the person giving the speech. It will not affect the grade of the person who delivered the speech.

5. The assignment will not be graded on punctuation, grammar, or spelling, but a well-written paper, using Standard English, is expected.

6. The length of the paper should be approximately two double-spaced typed pages.

Audience Analysis Exercise—Informative Speech

The Purpose

The purpose of this exercise is to gather and *apply* audience data to create a speech plan for an informative speech.

Audience Analysis Defined

An audience analysis is:

The process that involves gathering demographics about your listeners—such as age, sex, and occupation—and analyzing their psychological makeup, such as beliefs, group memberships, etc., then applying the data to ensure their interest in your speech.

The Assignment

Make a list of questions that pertain to your speech and that elicit information you would like to know about your audience. Ask these questions in class and record the answers. Listen carefully to other students' questions and the responses they receive as these may provide information you can use for your speech as well.

After collecting the audience data, write a paper (2–3 pages) that will explain how you are using specific audience data to make your speech effective for this audience. Your paper should include the following information:

- Your speech topic

- Your specific purpose statement, followed by an explanation of at least two facts you learned in your questioning that support this being an effective specific purpose for *this* audience.

- Your main points for the speech (usually 3–5), explaining why each point is essential, based on your audience data.

- The factors you will use to fulfill the audience's purpose in listening to you (WIFM), supporting them with audience data that indicate this would be effective.

- The factors that indicate what level of knowledge the audience has about your topic, again supported by your data. This section should explain and support how you are hitting your listeners at the correct level so you won't bore them or talk over their heads.

- The factors that indicate how you will be able to interest your listeners in your topic, supported by your data. This section includes factors that have helped you focus on ideas, techniques, and so on to keep them interested and listening to you.

- The type of informative speech you are going to be giving, including why you decided to approach the speech as demonstration, explanatory, or descriptive.
- An answer to the question, "Did you ask the 'right' questions?" Explain how your questions provided you with an adequate amount of information about your intended audience or what additional questions you wish you had asked to more effectively focus your speech for *this* audience.

Audience Analysis Exercise—Persuasive Speech

The Purpose

The purpose of this exercise is to gather and *apply* audience data to create a speech plan for a persuasive speech.

Audience Analysis Defined

An audience analysis is:

The process that involves gathering demographics about your listeners—such as age, sex, and occupation—and analyzing their psychological makeup, such as beliefs, group memberships, etc., then applying the data to ensure their interest in your speech.

The Assignment

Make a list of specific questions you would like to know about your audience that pertains to your speech. Ask these questions in class and record the answers. Listen carefully to other students' questions and the responses they receive as they may provide information you can use for your speech as well.

After collecting the audience data, write a paper (2–3 pages) that will explain how you are using specific audience data to make your speech effective for this audience. Your paper should include the following information:

- Your specific purpose statement worded correctly and written to reflect your ultimate persuasive goal.

- An overview of your introduction that shows how you will get attention, provide the topic, create WIFM, and establish your credibility. For each of these, you will need to explain what leads you to believe that approach will be effective for this specific audience, based on your audience data.

- What percentage of your audience:

  Is already doing what you want it to do or believe?

  Believes as you want it to, but isn't actively involved?

  Is fairly apathetic?

  Is leaning away from your position?

  Is definitely against your position?

- The main arguments/points of your speech (3–5), showing through your data that these are arguments that should be effective for this specific audience. Use the percentages you found (listed above) to help justify your choices.

- The type of evidence you will need for each of the arguments/points. Base this on what will be effective with this audience and explain your decisions through the use of your audience data. These will be your functional appeals.

- The type of emotional appeals that you will use in your speech. Explain why, from your data, these should be effective.

- For each of your main points, state whether you will be using a proposition of fact, value, or policy.

- An overview of your conclusion explaining how you will emphasize your ultimate goal and a clear call to action. Again, state why you believe this will be effective from your audience data.

Outline Format

Your Name
Class and Section #
Speech #

General Topic:
General Purpose:
Time Frame:
Specific Purpose Statement:

Introduction
   I.
  II.
 III.
 IV.
Body
   I.
      A.
      B.
  II.
      A.
         1.
         2.
            a.
            b.
      B.
      C.
 III.
      A.
      B.
Conclusion
   I.
  II.
Bibliography
   I.
  II.
 III.
 etc.

Please note that the number of Roman numerals, capital letters, Arabic numbers, and lowercase numbers will vary from this example, depending on your topic's specific breakdown in the outline. Otherwise you should label and follow this form as presented.

Persuasive Speaking Planner

Topic:

Audience Analysis:
What specifically do I need to know about my audience's attitudes, beliefs, and knowledge?

In what manner will I conduct my audience analysis?

I want my persuasive speech to be:

_____a. A speech to stimulate because my purpose is simply to increase and strengthen the attitudes and beliefs already held by my audience.

_____b. A speech to convince because my purpose is to convert the needs/ desires of my audience to my way of thinking.

_____c. A speech to activate because my purpose is to motivate my audience to take action.

My proposition is _____.

It is a proposition of

_____a. fact because my claim is that some objective belief is or isn't true.

_____b. value because my claim is that something is right or wrong or it works or doesn't work.

_____c. policy because my claim is that action must be taken and/or changed.

Organization:
How will I organize the body of my speech?

What organizational pattern will I use to get my points across?

Note: If I want to use the **Motivated Sequence** pattern (probably the best form of organization for persuasive speeches), I should answer the following questions:

How will I introduce my speech to get my audience member's attention and let them know what my subject is?

What audience needs will I address?

How will I provide the members of my audience with proof that there is a need for them to understand and agree with my claim?

How will I provide my audience with a solution to the established problem?

How will I get the members of my audience to see how much better it will be if they adopt my plan and how bad it will be if they don't?

How will I conclude my speech so my audience knows exactly what I want it to do?

My specific purpose is:

Evidence:
Use the following checklist to make sure your evidence is logical, ethical, and relevant.

_____ a. My reasoning does not include any fallacies.
_____ b. My claims are supported through my research.
_____ c. The organizational pattern I have used flows logically from point to point.
_____ d. I have accurately reported facts, statistics, and quotations.
_____ e. My sources are recent (within the past five years).
_____ f. My sources are unbiased as they relate to facts.
_____ g. Opinions are clearly labeled as such and the source is stated in my speech.
_____ h. My sources are relevant to my topic and proposition.

Speech Anxiety Analysis

1. What are the symptoms of speech anxiety you experience *before* presenting a speech?

2. How will you plan to cope with these symptoms before your next speech? For all of these symptoms listed in #1 devise a specific plan to eliminate, control, or mask them before your speech.

3. What are the symptoms of speech anxiety you actually experienced *during* your speech? Did you think CEM was an effective tool in overcoming them?

4. How will you plan to cope with the symptoms that did occur before your next speech? Use CEM to devise a specific plan to accomplish this.

Dealing with Speech Anxiety

1. Fill in the following blank: The thought of giving a speech makes me feel _____.

2. For five minutes continue writing about this idea. Don't worry about spelling, punctuation, and so on.

3. Share what you have written with the class and listen to what others have written.

4. You will find that many, if not most, of your classmates share many of the same anxieties as you. Discuss these ideas further and try to decide if they are logical. Come up with suggestions to help you and your classmates eliminate, control, or mask these anxieties. If any of your classmates said they had low anxiety, enlist their help by finding out how they came to feel this way.

Appendix B
Speech Evaluation Forms

Speech Evaluation Form 1

Speaker: Grade:

Speech Topic:

I. Delivery
   A. Eye contact
   B. Posture
   C. Gestures
   D. Facial expression
   E. Appearance
   F. Grammar
   G. Pronunciation
   H. Enunciation
   I. Tone
   J. Attitude toward audience and subject

II. Content
   A. Topic choice
   B. Organization
   C. Supporting material and bibliography
   D. Introduction
   E. Conclusion

III. Overall Impression:

Speech Evaluation Form 2

+ Place a *plus* in the blank if the speaker accomplished the item very effectively.

✓ Place a *check* in the blank if the speaker accomplished the item adequately.

– Place a *minus* in the blank if the speaker didn't accomplish the item.

Content

_____ 1. The goal (specific purpose) of the speech was clear.

_____ 2. The supportive information was credible and documented.

_____ 3. The speaker used a variety of material to present the topic.

_____ 4. Audio and/or visual aids were appropriate and well used.

_____ 5. The speaker adapted the content of the speech to the audience's interests, knowledge, and attitudes.

Organization

_____ 6. The introduction gained the attention of the audience while effectively leading into the speech.

_____ 7. The main points were clearly stated.

_____ 8. The transitions led smoothly from one point to another.

_____ 9. The conclusion summarized the main points of the speech.

Language

_____ 10. The language was easy to understand.

_____ 11. The language was vivid and descriptive.

_____ 12. The language was appropriate to the audience.

Delivery

_____ 13. The speaker sounded enthusiastic.

_____ 14. The speaker looked at all audience members.

_____ 15. The speaker showed sufficient vocal variety and emphasis.

_____ 16. Pronunciation and enunciation were correct.

_____ 17. The speaker used good posture.

_____ 18. The speaker's movements and gestures were appropriate.

_____ 19. The speaker's anxiety (if any) did not interfere with delivery.

Based on the criteria above, evaluate the speech as: (check one)

_____ excellent _____ good _____ satisfactory _____ fair _____ poor

Speech Evaluation Form 3

Name of Speaker_____ Date of Speech_____

Title of Speech_____ Length of Speech_____

The Speaker (circle the appropriate number):

1. Appearance sloppy	1 neat	2	3	4	5
2. Eye contact poor	1 effective	2	3	4	5
3. Voice: monotone	1 varied	2	3	4	5
4. Posture poor	1 correct	2	3	4	5
5. Gestures annoying	1 appropriate	2	3	4	5
6. Self-confidence nervous	1 poised	2	3	4	5

The Speech (check the appropriate blank and answer why):

A. Overall performance

1. The speaker's knowledge of the subject was carefully researched, without factual errors, and included details.

_____yes _____no   why?_____

2. The topic was relevant and suitable for this audience.

_____yes _____no   why?_____

3. The speaker's language wasn't too technical, filled with slang, or lacking description.

_____yes _____no   why?_____

4. The use of audio/visual aids was effective; they were appropriate in size, were handled with care, and added to, rather than interfered with, the speech.

_____yes _____no   why?_____

B. Parts of the speech

1. The introduction was appropriate, was attention getting, and provided the audience with a reason to listen.

_____yes _____no   why?_____

2. The body was organized, was well developed, and accomplished the goal of the speech.

_____yes   _____no   why?_____

3. The conclusion was effective, emphasized the main points of the speech, and tied everything together.

_____yes   _____no   why?_____

Reactions (briefly complete the following statements):

1. Of all the speakers today, this speaker should be ranked:

2. The speaker's main strengths were:

3. The speaker needs to improve on:

Appendix C
Vocal Exercises

To appreciate more fully the membrane called the diaphragm, get an ordinary balloon. Uninflated, the balloon's texture resembles the diaphragm itself without speech anxiety; it is resilient and pliable, yet remarkably strong (unless attacked with a pin or sharp object). (Remember that this membrane lies beneath the lungs and controls the volume of air permitted in the lungs.) Now blow up the balloon. As you perform this simple task of transferring air from your lungs to the balloon, notice how often you need to take a new breath to blow. Does the exchange of air in your lungs (i.e., inhaling and exhaling) take five to seven seconds or longer? Or are you more rapidly blowing up the balloon? The shorter the time for a complete breath (inhaling and exhaling), the shallower your breath, and the less lung capacity or potential capacity you are using. The inflated balloon resembles the texture of the diaphragm with speech anxiety—not too much give. With this exercise you have seen two things: the texture of the diaphragm and the capacity of your lungs.

Because air (in the form of breath) is the primary source of the sounds we make, let's look at the breathing process. To produce sounds successfully, we must know how to regulate and control the air flow. Here's the process. When we breathe, the following physical actions occur:

1. The muscles of the diaphragm tense, contract, and move downward, becoming more flat than domed.

2. This descending movement of the diaphragm compresses the stomach, liver, and kidneys, which causes a bulge in the abdominal walls.

3. The rib cage rises up and outward.

The preceding procedure causes the air pressure in the lungs to decrease, creating a partial vacuum so that air from outside rushes in to equalize the pressure.

As we reverse the process and exhale, the procedure reverses itself.

1. Relaxation of muscles allows the diaphragm to move upward (or we constrict the diaphragm, forcing air out of the lungs).

2. The stomach, liver, and kidneys return to their uncompressed positions.

3. The ribs then move down and inward due to the pull of gravity.

All of the above actions cause a decrease in the size of the chest cavity, which compresses the air in the lungs. This means that the air pressure in the lungs is now greater than the pressure outside the body and air is expelled through the mouth and nose.

In the absence of any physical respiratory problems, breathing (inhaling and exhaling) requires no conscious control or awareness. It is an automatic response of our body that keeps us alive. However, when we talk, we must be aware of what we are doing in order to control the breathing process consciously and produce effective, pleasing vocal tones.

When proper breathing techniques are used, the speaker inhales less frequently and will not have to gasp for breath because there will be a reserve of air. Longer phrases can be uttered, and jerky rhythms can be avoided. Furthermore, the larynx and throat will be less tense, which will improve vocal quality.

Correcting Extreme Upper-Chest Breathing

Purpose: The purpose of this exercise is to correct shallow breathing, which can interfere with effective speech.

Procedure:

1. Lie with your back flat on the floor. Place a book or pillow under your head, which will raise your head three-fourths to one inch. This places your head in the proper position for normal breathing.

2. Put your right hand on your abdomen and your left hand on the upper part of your chest above your sternum. Breathe as naturally as possible; inhale through your nose and exhale through your mouth or nose. Notice the expansion and contraction that occurs under your right hand and the little movement under your left hand. When you are aware of these movements, stand up and breathe in the same manner. Be careful not to lift your shoulders.

Yawning Exercise

Purpose: The purpose of this exercise is to feel the relaxation in the throat that will keep the voice from sounding tense.

Procedure:

1. Rest your tongue on the floor of your mouth and yawn.

2. Repeat several times. This will result in a reasonably relaxed throat.

3. Say "ah," continuing the sound for about five seconds. Don't let any tightness or tension enter your throat. If your throat begins to tense, discontinue the sound and repeat the yawn before attempting to vocalize again.

4. When you can sustain the sound for five seconds or more without tension, try the exercise by vocalizing each of the following sounds: "oo," "ee," "uh," "ou," "oh."

Alphabet Exercise

Purpose: The purpose of this exercise is to allow you to determine if your voice support is sufficient or if air is escaping unnecessarily.

Procedure:

1. Take a deep breath.
2. Without hurrying too much, try to say the alphabet in one breath. If you can't make it all the way through, you aren't breathing correctly. Don't strain. Relax. Easy does it.

Building Loudness

Purpose: The purpose of this exercise is to increase your volume by learning how to avoid excess air release.

Procedure:

1. Whisper the sound "ah."
2. Repeat the sound as you gradually build the volume, but avoid breathiness. Remember to breathe deeply and tense those inner throat muscles to keep the unvoiced airflow from leaking out.

Appendix D
Parliamentary Procedure

As early as the thirteenth century, with the signing of the Magna Carta, small groups began to take and control political power. With the rise of representative democracy in England, certain individuals were chosen to carry out the will of the majority regarding certain governmental practices. In order to accomplish this goal, specific rules of procedure evolved. You may have encountered the use of these rules in the organizational pattern of some of the clubs you have been a member of. These rules of procedure, which bear the name of the English representative body, Parliament, are based on democratic principles that allow all members of the group to state their opinions in an orderly fashion, leading to a thorough discussion of the issue at hand and, hopefully, a reasonable decision reached by the majority of those representatives present. It is upon this foundation that the framers of our Constitution based the legislative body of our nation. Parliamentary procedure is simple and efficient and is based on a standard agenda format (the order in which issues are discussed) and a set of guidelines for accomplishing the business at hand. This is the method employed by legislatures on state and national levels, and it is also employed by most civic, fraternal, and religious groups regardless of size.

When the term *parliamentary procedure* is mentioned, many students get a picture of some stuffy chamber where people are jumping to their feet, screaming phrases like "Point of order!" "Mr. Chairman, I had the floor!" or "Madame Chairman, I move to adjourn!" There would appear to be little organization here. But let's offer another scenario. Your group has assembled. The chairperson is at the podium. Following the basic agenda that follows, the first thing that happens is the chairperson calls for the meeting to begin: the call to order. Assuming the group has met before and has selected a secretary to record the actions of the assembled body, we then have the reading of those actions, called the minutes of the previous meeting. After the secretary has read the minutes, the chairperson will state: "If there are no additions or corrections, the minutes will stand approved as read." The meeting then proceeds through each section of the agenda, pausing as need be for questions or motions from the floor concerning the topics brought up before the group. Each meeting is different. Sometimes emotional issues are presented and discussed heatedly. But order can be maintained and business can be accomplished when members respect each other's rights to be heard and maintain relevancy.

Sample Agenda

The standard form for the agenda is as follows:

1. Call to order
2. Reading of the minutes of the previous meeting
3. Treasurer's report
4. Reports from committees

5. Old business (any topic previously discussed by the group)

6. New business

7. Announcements

8. Adjournment

Motions

The business accomplished during the use of parliamentary procedure takes the form of motions, which are statements by any member of the group, after recognition by the chairperson, of action that the member would like taken by the group. The proper words for introduction of a motion are "I move . . . ," never, "I make a motion"!

The steps for a passage of a motion are as follows:

1. Motion is made.

2. Motion is seconded. (Another member says it ought to be done.)

3. Discussion is held. (Here, both sides of the issue are investigated; amendments are perhaps added at this time.)

4. Vote is taken.

5. Results of the vote are announced by the chairperson.

It might be appropriate to elaborate here on the role of the chairperson. He or she must keep the goals of the organization in focus and free from his or her individual bias. It is not an easy role to play, but with experience and sound judgment, the chairperson can lead the group to significant accomplishments through mutual effort and understanding.

Now, we offer a word about the record keeper, the secretary. This is the person whose responsibility it is to keep an accurate ongoing record of the business being discussed (for an example of minutes see the next section). He or she will not be able to remember everything, so careful note-taking skills are essential. The person designated as secretary may feel it necessary to tape the proceedings and base the written minutes on that audiotape. It is part of the organizing plan of parliamentary procedure to have an accurate record of the proceedings. For a hands-on experience with parliamentary procedure, your instructor may wish to employ the following exercise.

Panel Discussion

Purpose: This exercise will give you experience in working in groups aimed toward a goal. As the discussions are presented, the class can be turned into a meeting run by parliamentary procedure.

Procedure:

Split the class into groups of three to five persons. A leader may be designated or decided on by the group. Have the groups assemble and choose a topic of local, state, national, or international interest (a local tax proposal, building renovations, abortion laws, foreign aid, terrorists, etc.). Allow the groups to go out and gather information on the topic, choosing a specific area for each person to cover. For example, if the topic is abortion, one person might take the subject of sterilization procedures; another might cover the psychology of the woman involved in an abortion. Each person will be responsible for a five-minute talk on his or her topic. The chairperson of the group will introduce the topic, define terms, and, at the end of the presentation, propose a motion for action of the class as a whole. When the proposal (motion) is seconded and discussion begins, the entire class may ask questions to clarify the issues discussed. The motion is then voted upon and the results announced. (See the steps for passage of a motion above.) Assign a member of the class who is not on the panel to take minutes of the meeting and discussion, which will be read at the following class meeting. A sample of minutes appears below.

Sample Minutes

Panel Discussion I
March 24, 2009

Call to Order:	9:30 AM
Roll Call:	Susan Black, Chairperson
	Tom Dean
	Julie Bequette
Committee Report:	Space Exploration/The Final Frontier?

A report was given by the panel mentioned above on the past, present, and future of the United States Space Program. Americans spend more money on cigarettes, liquor, and travel than the government spends on the entire Space Program.

Our society has been affected by the advances made in the Space Program. For instance, modern space suits were designed to be lightweight and waterproof, thus giving someone the idea to make a disposable diaper to keep wetness away from the baby. Also, space suits were flame retardant, giving yet another individual the inspiration to create children's clothing and blankets that are flame retardant.

Some other advancements not discussed in great detail were: communication satellites, medicine, and weather.

"The accomplishments of the Space Program must be evaluated in decades, not by cost."

We were left with one final thought: "What is our future in space?"

Proposal:	A motion and a second that there be a special section on the Federal Income Tax Form to give individuals the opportunity to donate to the Space Program. Carried.
Announcements:	There will be another Panel Discussion on Thursday, March 26, 2009.
Adjournment:	10:20 AM

Appendix E
Small Group
Exercises and
Evaluation Forms

Problem-Solving Discussion

Objectives: There are several reasons for this project:

1. Learn and demonstrate effective small group process
2. Become more *information literate* through researching a topic
3. Provide data for the audience on a chosen topic
4. Demonstrate effective delivery skills

Format: Your group should use the following format in presenting your discussion:

1. Provide an introduction that states the problem in the form of a problem statement, gains the audience's attention, and provides a reason(s) why the audience will benefit from the discussion.
2. Define any necessary terms that will be used in the discussion in order to provide common understanding.
3. Give a history of the problem: when it began, why, significant events, dates, legislation, and so on—anything that the audience needs to understand.
4. Explain several solutions for the problem, discussing the pros and cons of each.
5. Present the group's solution in the form of a plan and discuss why, according to your group's consensus, this is the best approach to solving the problem.
6. Call the audience to support the group's solution through specific action in your conclusion.

Additional Information: The following information is necessary for satisfactorily completing the assignment:

1. The discussion should take most of the class time on the scheduled presentation day.
2. You must include support for what is presented during the discussion by establishing evidence through your research.
3. A bibliography in standard form must be presented to the instructor on the day of your discussion.
4. You must take questions and comments from your audience. This may be done during the discussion or in a question/answer period following the group's presentation. On your scheduled presentation day, you will be asked when you want to have a question period.
5. While an outline is not required for this assignment, a general format may be useful for each member of your group to have as a guideline.

6. Remember, this is a discussion, not a debate or a series of individual speeches all related to one topic. While the topic may be broken down and assigned to different members of the group for research purposes, this is interactive and all members should be presenting information and comments throughout the entire discussion.

7. There is nothing wrong with creativity. Your objective is to persuade your listeners that your topic is a problem and your solution needs their action. Find the most effective way of doing this.

Group Analysis Form

Group Climate

Each of the statements below refers to a different aspect of group climate. In one of the five spaces at the right of each statement, place a check mark to indicate your best estimate of that aspect in your group.

Aspect of Group Climate	Outstanding	Superior	Average	Poor	Unsatisfactory
Pleasantness: Everyone seems to enjoy the group.					
Security: Members feel safe speaking; neither ideas nor people are ridiculed.					
Cohesion: Members support one another, stick up for the group, avoid outside disruptive forces.					
Purposefulness: Goals are understood at the start and kept in mind throughout.					
Objectivity: Members are critical of prejudice and avoid it, seek the best solutions to a problem.					
Involvement: Members are eager to participate and do so.					

(continued)

Aspect of Group Climate	Outstanding	Superior	Average	Poor	Unsatisfactory
Cooperativeness: Members contribute to the best of their ability; there is little fighting for status and personal goals.					
Communication: Remarks seem addressed to everyone; no cliques form; chair doesn't talk to only a few.					
Permissiveness: Members are not autocratic; group makes most decisions; atmosphere is relaxed, accepting, and informal.					
Productivity: Members keep at the job and produce effectively.					
Integrativeness: Group involves all members readily; utilizes all resources, not just a few.					
Flexibility: Group adjusts to changing needs; benefits from mistakes.					

Contributions

List the name of each participant in your group (include yourself) above a column. Then in the appropriate box, indicate how often each member acted as indicated in the first column. Use the following scale to denote the frequency:

4 = Often
3 = Occasionally
2 = Seldom
1 = Never

Participants:

Contributes							
Gives information							
Asks for information							
Gives opinions							
Defines, clarifies or shows relationships							
Asks for definitions, clarification, or relationships							
Argues or refutes (supported)							
Argues or refutes (unsupported)							
Supports others, praises, defends							
Releases tension, jokes, shows satisfaction							
Shows tension, withdraws, blocks or attacks others							

Group Roles

Who do you believe was the leader in your group? Why do you think so? Was this person an effective leader—why or why not?

What task roles were taken on by individual members of your group? Who did what?

What maintenance roles were taken on by individual members of your group? Who did what?

What personal roles emerged and in which members of your group? How did they affect the group as a whole?

Glossary

adrenaline   A hormone produced by the body under stress resulting in a boost in energy.

antilistening behaviors   Behaviors that result when we give in to distractions and may occur if we have not had any formal training in listening, or when we are taught not to listen.

appearance   A nonverbal element that gives the audience an impression of you based on how you look.

articulation   The process of forming clear, individual sounds that are distinctly spoken words.

assumptions   The belief that we have heard the information before, that we know what the speaker will say, that the message is insignificant, or that the information is just not applicable to us.

attending   The second step in the listening process that consists of trying to pay attention to the sounds we hear.

audience analysis   The process that involves: (1) gathering demographics about your listeners—such as age, sex, and occupation, (2) analyzing listeners' psychological makeup, group memberships, etc., and (3) applying the data to ensure their interest in your speech.

audio clip   A recording that enhances your speech and resonates with the audience.

audio/visual aids   Such devices as posters, pictures, charts, PowerPoints, and recordings that are used by the speaker to add interest to a speech and aid in getting his or her speech across to the audience.

authority   Refers to an author or information provider who is an individual and/or an organization, possessing experience and/or knowledge that qualifies him/her/it as a valid source of information.

bias   A political or ideological preference that is stated or implied.

bibliography   A list of sources in alphabetical order; there is a standard form for the information listed in the bibliography—often MLA or APA.

bibliography card   A card that contains the necessary information for each source.

blackboard   A board on which you can make quick drawings or charts during your speech.

brainstorming   Collecting many ideas quickly as they occur to you, without analyzing each one.

call to action   Requesting the audience to perform an action that relates to a persuasive appeal.

causal organization   Outline progression organized to show cause-and-effect relationships.

CEM   An acronym that stands for "control, eliminate, and mask"; a process that can help you control your anxiety, eliminate symptoms of it, and mask nervous behaviors during speaking.

channel   The medium through which a message travels to reach its audience.

chronological organization   Outline progression organized by time occurrence.

cognitive dissonance theory   Suggests that inconsistencies create discomfort or conflict, which then creates a need to restore consistency or comfort.

cohesiveness   The ability to function as a group and achieve the group's goals by putting aside individual gratification.

collectivism   A theory that promotes the idea that the needs of the group supersede those of each individual.

committees   Groups formed to accomplish a specific purpose for a determined amount of time, generally labeled according to the group's reason for meeting.

communication   A free exchange of thoughts, feelings, and ideas.

communicator   A person involved in exchanging messages with one or more other people.

compromise   A decision where some members must abandon their opinions in favor of what works for the group as a whole.

conclusion   The last part of the speech, which summarizes your main points, links back to the introduction, and notifies the audience you are finished.

conflict management   A form of group process widely used at the corporate level in which members meet collectively to bargain and negotiate final decisions on various issues.

conflict resolution   Coming up with strategies to deal with conflicting interests or perspectives so a group can function effectively.

consensus   Coming to a decision when all members of the group unanimously agree on an issue.

content   The breadth and depth of the material supplied.

credibility   An audience's perception of you as trustworthy based on your knowledge of the subject and your personal appearance.

crisis situation   A form of group process in which group members are required to assess a situation and make decisions based on limited information.

currency   Reference to the age of the information being used.

decoding   Translating verbal and/or nonverbal symbols into mental images.

delivery   The process of presenting your information to an audience.

demographic data   Measurable statistics such as age, income, and gender about audience members; used in audience analysis.

demonstration speech   Type of informative speech that shows the steps necessary to take a process from beginning to end.

descriptive speech   Type of informative speech that uses words to paint a clear picture of a person, place, or thing.

design   The layout of a Web site.

diaphragm   A muscle located under the rib cage.

digital presentation   Displaying information by using computers, software, and projectors.

do-it-aller   The person who takes control of the group and insists everything be done his or her way, by him or her alone.

emotional appeals   Used in persuasive speeches to make a plea to the feelings of the audience.

encoding   Translating mental images into symbols.

enunciation   The act of pronouncing individual vowel and consonant sounds.

ethics   A system that entails honesty; it guides speakers to convey accurate information.

evaluating   The third step in the listening process where we attempt to understand what is being communicated to us and determine its familiarity and/or importance to us.

evidence   Anything created and substantiated by another person that is not your personal opinion.

explanatory speech   A type of informative speech that provides a clear explanation of a complex issue or idea.

extemporaneous delivery   The kind of speech prepared and practiced from an outline, not memorized or read from a manuscript, resulting in a more "personal" delivery to the audience.

external elements (noise)   Distractions that occur outside the body and interfere with the listening process.

eye contact   Facing and meeting the audience's eyes with your own.

facial expressions   Animation of the speaker's face that conveys to the audience how the speaker feels.

fallacies   Statements that are not valid or logical and should be avoided when giving a speech.

fear   A persuasive technique that uses the audience's apprehension to motivate them.

feedback   The constant exchange of verbal and/or nonverbal messages between communicators.

fillers   Ineffective words or sounds, such as "um" and "like," which weaken the speaker's delivery.

flipchart   A big tablet of paper propped on an easel at a meeting.

fluidity   The ease and smoothness of verbal delivery.

focusing   The process of narrowing your speech to reflect what effect it will have on the target audience.

formal outline   A document that arranges material in an orderly and easy-to-follow format, according to certain rules; final outline often submitted.

freeloader   Any group member who does not participate in the group process but expects to reap the benefits of the group.

functional appeals   Used in persuasive speeches to make a plea based on factual information.

general conversation   Any conversation occurrence that could produce a possible subject/topic for a speech.

general topic   The starting point of any speech; the theme or subject of a speech.

gestures   The movement of hand(s) or body to add emphasis to important points in the speech.

grabber   An interesting way of gaining the audience's attention, and the first part of the introduction.

grammar   The system of word structure and arrangement for language.

habits   Behaviors we engage in consistently but don't pay attention to.

handout   A copy of information related to or in your speech that you can give to each audience member.

hearing   The reverberation of sound waves in the ear.

hitchhiking   Building off of topics/subjects in a list to generate additional topics/subjects.

impromptu speech   A spontaneous, unprepared speech, usually given on the spur of the moment without any prior notice.

individualism   A theory that promotes the belief that the interests of individuals should take precedence over those of the state.

informative speech   That speech form whose main purpose is to increase the audience's knowledge about a particular subject.

internal noise   Distractions that occur inside the body that interfere with the listening process.

Internet   An intangible place where you can obtain information (such as on Web sites) and communicate with people via computers that have the hardware, software, and service provider needed to enable access; also known as the Net and the Web.

Internet address   A way of locating sources on the Net. Each Web site has its own unique URL (address) that must be entered into a Web browser to access the site.

interview   A research method by which you question someone and record his or her answers.

intrapersonal communication   The communication inside your own head; the "voice" in your head. It can be a cause of not listening.

introduction   The first section of a public speech that presents the topic, gains attention, and connects the speaker to the audience.

language   A written or spoken system of symbols that is used to convey a message.

larynx   Contains the membranes known as vocal chords.

leader   The person who facilitates the achievements and tasks of the group, by inspiring trust, listening to others' ideas, and attempting to understand others' opinions.

lecture   Type of informative speech that is a structured, lengthy presentation usually used in educational settings.

library catalog   A list of all the sources in the library.

listening   An active willingness of a communicator to not only hear but also understand a speaker.

logic   The orderly succession of evidence leading to an understandable conclusion.

maintenance roles   Group roles that help cement group cohesiveness.

majority rule   Decision-making process that requires 51 percent or more of the group vote.

manuscript delivery   A speech where the speaker reads either from a paper text or off a teleprompter.

media   Radio, TV, newspapers, magazines, DVDs, CDs, the Internet—the methods of distributing or transmitting information.

memorized delivery   A speech that is not read word for word but is recited from memory; an ineffective delivery style because sometimes the speaker forgets or repeats an item.

message   An idea, thought, or emotion transmitted from one person to another.

message overload   Excessive amounts of information that saturate our brains and cause us not to listen.

microphone   a device you might use when speaking to a large group, but that you need to check before you give your speech to make sure it is working properly.

model   A pictorial representation of an idea or concept.

modeling theory   Asserts that using examples that the audience views positively increases the probability of motivating your audience to model or accept your viewpoint.

Monroe's Motivated Sequence   A five-step process created by Alan Monroe in the 1930s and used to organize an effective persuasive speech.

needs   The physical and psychological factors that human beings rely on; desires that motivate choices in human beings and are the basis of a persuasive speech.

noise   Physical or psychological barriers—internal or external—to the accurate sending or receiving of a message; distractions.

nonverbal elements   Elements of communication that are not language specific: eye contact, gestures, tone of voice, and so on.

object   An item that is the exact, real one about which you are speaking.

occasion   Event or purpose for which a speech is given.

organize   The act of deciding three to five main points that will be addressed in your speech.

organizational pattern   Way of dividing and ordering your main points so that your speech will move from point to point in a logical and easily understood progression.

outlining   Organizing and arranging your material in a way that is orderly and easy to follow.

overhead projector   A machine that uses a transparency to bounce an image onto a screen, where it is magnified and easily seen by audience members.

pauses   The time between sounds or words.

periodicals   Publications such as magazines, newspapers, and journals that are printed and distributed at regular intervals throughout the year.

personal environment   The total experience pattern, background, and value scheme from which a person thinks, acts, and speaks.

personal experience   The knowledge you've accumulated during your lifetime, which can be a good starting point for a speech.

personal roles   Those individualistic and self-centered roles that frustrate the group's ability to achieve its task.

persuasive speech   The type of speech that attempts to produce some change in attitude or behavior in an audience, and attempts to gain agreement from the audience to adopt the speaker's viewpoint.

pertinent information   Other sources that expand on and/or enhance a primary source of information.

picture   A visual image that helps the audience understand your material by "seeing" it.

pitch   Refers to range, or where a sound would be placed on a musical scale.

plagiarism   The use of another person's work without giving credit to that person.

popular vote   Decision process that chooses the item that is the most popular with group members.

poster   A professional-looking display of information that can be made on a computer.

posture   The manner in which the speaker holds his or her body.

practice   Rehearsal of a speech.

preoccupied   Absorbed with our own thoughts.

primary groups   Groups that exist for the long term, such as family.

primary source   The source you believe is the most comprehensive.

priority organization   Separates items by importance, least to most important or the reverse.

problem solution organization   Outline progression that poses a problem and then offers a solution.

process organization   An outline progression that organizes material according to a series of step-by-step actions.

pronunciation   Separating and accenting syllables in the correct manner.

proposition of fact   Persuasive argument that proposes that something is factual.

proposition of policy   Persuasive argument that proposes a course of action.

proposition of value   Persuasive argument that proposes that something is right or wrong.

proximity   Refers to the use of current examples, events, quotes, or occurrences, lending to their credibility.

psychological data   Measurable information about the morals, values, beliefs, and lifestyles of your audience members; used in audience analysis.

rate   The speed at which your words are delivered.

reference works   Research sources such as encyclopedias, dictionaries, and almanacs.

reinforcement theory   Theory that suggests that behavior can be changed by pointing out rewards or consequences of adopting a particular viewpoint.

relevancy   How a topic or supportive item corresponds to your topic and audience.

report   Type of informative speech used in a business setting that addresses a specific purpose or topic.

research   The process of gathering information for your speech, which may include quotations, statistics, or examples; research supports your ideas and gives the audience a reason to believe you.

research notes   Notes used for organizing your research work.

research plan   Guideline for researching that addresses what information you need, why you need it, and where to find it.

responding   Final step in the listening process in which we send a speaker a message that indicates we have received his or her message; also known as feedback.

retaining   Step 4 in the listening process, which relies on memory to recall information.

secondary groups   Groups formed for a short period of time to complete a specific task.

semantics   The meaning of words.

sensory mode   How we comprehend new information; often this mode is visual.

significance   Considering how the supportive examples, studies, and other forms of information you choose directly relate to or affect your speech.

singular motive   A form of group process in which all members of the group collectively pursue the same goal or specific task.

small group communication   Working collectively with others; a group that consists of three to fifteen people who interact for the purpose of attaining specific goals.

spatial organization   Outline progression that organizes material according to geographical space or area arrangement.

speaking environment   The third element of your working plan, consisting of the facility and general area in which you will address your audience.

speaking outline   The outline you take to the podium.

special occasion speech   A speech designed to keep the audience's attention and interest for a short period of time, usually at some special event.

specific purpose   Being clear about the result of your speech.

specific purpose statement   A single sentence that states the response the speaker wishes the audience to have at the end of the speech.

specific task   A goal that is collectively pursued by a small group.

specific topic   The result of the focusing process; a narrowed or "specific" topic.

speech anxiety   The physical and psychological (often unfounded) apprehension or fear of a public performance, including giving a speech.

speech notes   (1) The notes the speaker actually takes to the podium. (2) The notes you may use and adjust when you practice your speech.

speech process   The nine steps that incorporate and summarize the concepts, skills, and practices that make a speech effective.

speech to activate   A type of persuasive speech that asks the audience's participation in some action.

speech to convince   A type of persuasive speech that converts the audience to the speaker's viewpoint.

speech to stimulate   A type of persuasive speech that increases beliefs already held by the audience.

speech topic   An idea that interests you and that you can talk about that won't require mountains of research to support.

stage fright   Opening-night jitters suffered by professional actors and sometimes experienced when speaking in public.

suitability   Material that is appropriate for your audience and that supports your stance or explains your topic.

surveys   Instruments designed to gather factual data or opinions from a large number of people by asking questions about a specific topic.

symbol   A mental image.

synergy   The concept that the combination of the parts has more value than each part working alone; 1 + 1 = 3.

task roles   Group roles that help the group organize and accomplish set goals.

tone   The combined vocal elements of rate, pitch, and volume.

transition   A word or phrase used to shift from one point to another, such as *however*, *for example*, and *in addition*.

variety   The use of many different kinds of support such as examples, quotations, statistics, research conclusions, and visual aids within the context of a speech.

verbal elements   Words and language that represent images and ideas used to deliver a speech.

video   A visual aid that helps the audience understand your material by "seeing" it.

vocals   The sounds we make.

voice   A combination of elements such as tone, rate, pitch, and volume that, depending on how you use them, affect the verbal delivery of your speech.

volume   The loudness or softness of the tones produced when sound resonates in your sinus cavities.

whiteboard   A board on which you can make quick drawings or charts during your speech.

WIFM   An acronym that stands for "what's in it for me"; gives the audience a reason to listen to you.

wiki   Document collaboration writing software.

working plan   Defines and incorporates your audience analysis with what you know about your occasion and speaking environment.

working outline   Organizational tool used by a speaker during the early speech preparation period to decide the most effective order for presentation.

Index